WALKING DISTANCE

Walking Distance

*Remembering Classic Episodes
from Classic Television*

Victor L. Cahn

RESOURCE *Publications* · Eugene, Oregon

WALKING DISTANCE
Remembering Classic Episodes from Classic Television

Copyright © 2014 Victor L. Cahn. All rights reserved. Except for brief quotations in critical publications or reviews, no part of this book may be reproduced in any manner without prior written permission from the publisher. Write: Permissions, Wipf and Stock Publishers, 199 W. 8th Ave., Suite 3, Eugene, OR 97401.

Resource Publications
An Imprint of Wipf and Stock Publishers
199 W. 8th Ave., Suite 3
Eugene, OR 97401

www.wipfandstock.com

ISBN 13: 978-1-62564-794-8

Manufactured in the U.S.A.

07/16/2014

To
my brother, Dr. Steven M. Cahn,
and
my sister-in-law, Marilyn Ross (Cahn), M.D.

Contents

    Introduction | ix

    Prologue | 1

I   *The Twilight Zone:* "Walking Distance" | 5

II   *The Phil Silvers Show (You'll Never Get Rich):* "The Court Martial"
     and
   McHale's Navy: "Dear Diary" | 24

III *Maverick:* "Shady Deal at Sunny Acres"
     and
   The Fugitive: "Nightmare at Northoak" | 43

IV *The Dick Van Dyke Show:* "Baby Fat"
     and
   The Andy Griffith Show: "Man in a Hurry" | 69

V   *The Avengers:* "Escape in Time"
     and
   Get Smart: "Casablanca" | 94

VI *The Honeymooners:* "The Golfer"
     and
   All in the Family: "Judging Books By Their Covers" | 121

    Epilogue | 147

    Works Cited | 149

    Index | 151

    About the Author | 161

Introduction

Every generation has its own cultural heritage. For tens of millions who came of age during the 1950s and 60s, and who will forever bear the title "Baby Boomers," the bedrock of that heritage is television.

This phenomenon began at the mid-point of the twentieth century, and combined the immediacy of radio with the endurance of film. Like radio, television offered daily and weekly programs that were broadcast into our homes, where we could enjoy them either in solitude or amidst our families. Like movies, television provided pictures that made such experiences indelible.

How much impact do these shows retain?

One measure is the number from that era which today are presented as frequently as ever. Indeed, on stations like "ION Television," "TV Land," and "MeTV," reruns from forty, fifty, and sixty years ago are the staple of their fare, while many other cable networks profitably fill their hours with these same shows.

Even more telling, however, are the countless images and sounds that remain touchstones for those who watched and listened decades ago.

A few notes of the opening theme to *Perry Mason* are all boomers need to conjure up memories of Raymond Burr as the dauntless attorney along with the show's other regulars: Barbara Hale as secretary Della Street, William Hopper as detective Paul Drake, William Talman as DA Hamilton Burger, and Ray Collins as Lieutenant Tragg (whose first name, for trivia buffs, happened to be "Arthur").

The phrase "a three-hour tour" heralds the ballad of *Gilligan's Island*, with Bob Denver as the hapless mate, Alan Hale, Jr. as the Skipper, Jim Backus and Natalie Schaeffer as Mr. and Mrs. Howell, and the rest of the marooned passengers. No doubt the discussion will quickly turn to the ever-raging question as to which female castaway was more desirable: Ginger or Mary Ann?

Introduction

"Lucy, you got some serious 'splainin' to do." The speaker could only be Desi Arnaz as Ricky Ricardo on *I Love Lucy*, demanding the truth from his madcap wife played by real-life spouse Lucille Ball.

I could cite many more.

But such early programs remain beloved not just because they evoke what may seem a more innocent time. In fact, children and young adults enjoy them as much as their parents and grandparents still do.

The more important reason is that these shows were superbly crafted. The writers, directors, producers, and actors who worked under the strictures of that day were compelled to use their ingenuity, and the best of their creations remain terrific comedies and dramas that will please audiences in perpetuity.

Too often, though, the shows are dismissed as mere "entertainment" unworthy of serious study. Even to some loyal viewers, a line-by-line dissection of a script from *The Honeymooners* or *The Fugitive* may seem incongruous. But one aim of this book is to confirm that like quality movies, novels, and plays, these programs merit detailed analysis. Moreover, such a process teaches not only how great art is constructed, but also how it may impact our lives.

In the following essays, I probe with what I like to think is singular depth into individual episodes from eleven shows. I don't claim that these are the absolute best from that era, although some surely are. The ones considered here, however, mattered most to me. The opening chapter is devoted to "Walking Distance" from *The Twilight Zone,* and each of the next five sections considers two shows that are in some way related and therefore deserve to be explored in tandem. I hope that all together they represent a proper selection of style and spirit.

I also hope that my retrospective will inspire readers, even those who know these programs well, to revisit them and enjoy them even more.

Prologue

I was born in 1948. During the same year, the family's first television came into our home, and soon the set and I became a team.

Ever since I was old enough to walk and carry a tray bearing food, I have relished retreating alone into a room and peacefully eating while I watch television. Fortunately my family indulged my predilection, so during the 50s and 60s I enjoyed more than my share of private viewing. Of the many shows I liked, some actually shaped how I looked at the world, and in this book I explain why.

The first programs I watched regularly were . . . and I'm not kidding . . . soap operas. My pre-kindergarten classes ended at 12:00 PM, at which time I was driven home by bus. If I was among the first to be dropped off, I could see *Love of Life* at 12:15. If I arrived a little later, I started with *Search for Tomorrow* at 12:30. And if I was among the last to be deposited, I had to be satisfied with only one show: *The Guiding Light* at 12:45.

I knew the names of all the characters and actors. I followed the complex plots, and I worried about the outcomes.

I was four.

The first primetime show that earned my regular attention was *The Adventures of Superman*, starring George Reeves as the Man of Steel (although I never referred to him as such). I bought the illusion of his flying, and I enjoyed the last-minute rescues, but certain details bothered me. First, almost every time Superman prepared for action, his alter ego, Clark Kent, would dash into the same store room at the Daily Planet building to change into his costume. Why, I wondered, did no one notice this quirk? Second, I could never understand why when crooks shot bullets at Superman, he stood tall, arms akimbo, and invited the assault, but after his foes exhausted their ammunition and threw their guns, he ducked. Wouldn't the empty weapons have just bounced off him? Most of all, Clark and Superman looked so much alike. Couldn't anyone make the connection?

I also observed that two women played Lois Lane: first Phyllis Coates, then Noel Neill. Both were attractive and capable, but Coates was tougher, and did not hesitate to belittle Clark when he failed to meet her standards for male behavior. Frankly, she scared me. Jack Larsen as young Jimmy Olsen and John Hamilton as Editor Perry White were both likeable, although I sensed that Mr. White's grouchy exterior masked affection for his reporters. In some episodes Olsen and White were almost buddies, but in others Jimmy's antics pushed Mr. White to the end of his tether. I could never see any consistency to their relationship.

My favorite part of each show was the closing, when Clark or Superman would either comment on how everyone had been fooled, or offer a point of wisdom that we should ponder. At the end of one episode, for instance, someone asked Superman how he knew that Jimmy had been in danger. "Oh, I was just flying by," he answered, with a knowing wink to the camera (and me). In another, Clark resurfaced just after Superman had flown away, and Lois became suspicious. "I wonder," she mused. "No wonder," replied Clark. "You're a pretty *wonderful* girl."

Lois winced, but I thought the pun was clever.

When George Reeves died in 1957, possibly by suicide, possibly as a victim of foul play (we still don't know), I understood that he was an actor playing a part and not the real thing. Thus I was spared the trauma that afflicted countless other youngsters.

By that time, however, his place in my pantheon had been usurped by two other heroes, both the product of Walt Disney Studios. The first was Davy Crockett, whose popularity was a craze of national proportions. Like most children, I sang his theme song: "Born on a mountain top in Tennessee . . ." but unlike most, I memorized all the verses. On the other hand, I had no interest in acquiring my own copy of Davy's famous coonskin cap. Too many other people wore them.

I enjoyed the original three episodes that concluded at the Alamo, where fortunately we never saw Davy die. But I enjoyed even more the follow-up stories: Davy's adventures with Mike Fink, in which they raced keelboats and battled river pirates. Fess Parker became one of my favorite actors, and after the Crockett series ended I was happy to see him play a much different role, that of a Union spy during the Civil War in Disney's 1956 film *The Great Locomotive Chase*.

My third hero was Zorro, who wore an all-black costume and mask as he swash-buckled his way through the early days of California, protecting

Prologue

the poor and helpless from the evil designs of the military governor. Like Superman, Zorro (Guy Williams) had a secret identity as Don Diego, a dandy who was as timid as Zorro was courageous, but he also had a confederate: his mute servant, Bernardo (Gene Sheldon). Later Don Diego's father learned the secret. Thus Zorro never underwent the crisis of loneliness that I assumed Superman must have endured. Surely the man who could leap tall buildings in a single bound wanted to tell everybody, *somebody*, look who I am! Zorro, however, seemed to be spared such angst. So taken was I with his prowess that when school was out and I could dress according to my own tastes, I took to wearing a black sports shirt and black trousers, another whim my family indulged.

By the mid-1950s my interests began to broaden, and soon they encompassed many more shows, especially the ones discussed here. But before I begin my in-depth reflections, a few additional comments are in order.

First, I almost never watched traditional children's programs, especially those that featured gangs of kids packed tightly in studio bleachers. Nor did I enjoy supposedly grow-up shows that focused on youngsters who tossed out snappy one-liners. Some programs I favored had children in the cast, but they were rarely the core of the action, and when they were I was bored. Even as a little boy, I wanted to watch adults functioning in the adult world. I had my own difficulties dealing with school and the characters therein, so seeing similar problems on television did not interest me. Besides, I couldn't identify with anyone who uttered any version of "Gee, that'll be neat!"

Second, and at the risk of being obvious, I must note that these shows depicted a world that today seems antediluvian. The web did not exist. No one had a cell phone or a personal computer (I omit, of course, science fiction programs and spy spoofs). Compact discs and DVDs were unknown, as were forerunners like cassettes, and home phones did not have answering attachments. On the other hand, an awful lot of people smoked cigarettes, and plenty of husbands donned ties and jackets to putter around the house.

Furthermore, scripts were governed by strict rules, so scenes of violence were measured, and sexual acts more intimate than kissing were essentially forbidden. Plots were censored ruthlessly by networks and sponsors, and material that we now consider "mature" did not survive. Language had to be free of street slang and crude exclamations, and anatomical features and functions were never mentioned. Of course, no cable programming was available to test such regulations.

WALKING DISTANCE

Minority characters were rare. Married women functioned solely at home, while single women with careers usually longed to marry, then function solely at home.

Third, only three national networks were available, plus a scattering of local channels, and broadcasts everywhere were technically primitive. Sometimes a few cameras were used, but often only one was employed, and special effects were nil.

Despite these obstacles, however, quality shows emerged.

Finally, given the devotion that will be apparent from the following analyses, television may seem to have been my sole occupation. Not at all. I practiced the violin daily, completed schoolwork on time, and played sports and games at every opportunity.

I was also a dedicated reader. I consumed some fiction, but preferred history and biography. In retrospect, I realize that back then I read to learn more about the world around me, but when I wanted to escape that world, I sought drama. Occasionally (very occasionally when I was a child) I attended plays. A bit more frequently I went to the movies. Much more frequently I watched television. In other words, I enjoyed theater in every form, and television was the vehicle most readily available. Small wonder, then, that I became a playwright, an actor, and an English professor who specialized in dramatic literature.

Let me conclude with a few words about the programs I've chosen.

The majority are light-hearted, but I have always enjoyed comedy most, and when I was young my tastes were already formed.

I omit game shows such as *To Tell the Truth, I've Got a Secret, What's My Line, Beat the Clock, College Bowl, Stump the Stars* (also known as "Pantomime Quiz"), and *You Bet Your Life* with Groucho Marx. These were dramatic but in a different way. They were also personality-driven, not script-driven, and thus not suitable for examination here. For the same reason I have excluded talk shows, specifically *The Tonight Show*, first with Jack Paar (when Steve Allen hosted, I was too young to stay awake), then with Johnny Carson.

My focus in each essay is on a representative sample from each series, but within these close readings (or viewings) my scope encompasses other episodes, as well as peripheral matters that I hope prove intriguing. Fortunately all these programs are available on DVD or the web, so I need not rely on memory alone.

Here, then, are the choice television shows of my youth, now to be savored again.

I

The Twilight Zone

"Walking Distance"

Let's begin with a couple of my unshakeable convictions.
One, *The Twilight Zone* is the most influential program in the history of television.

Two, "Walking Distance" is not only the best episode of that series, but the most eloquent half-hour from any series. True, I haven't seen every program ever broadcast; nevertheless, I stand by my claim.

Now let's proceed.

First to the show in general, which as much as any work of popular entertainment is embedded in our national consciousness. The title remains a byword for the mysterious or bizarre, and any sounding of its four-note motif immediately suggests that something unnerving looms over, around, under, or within us. Even a meager imitation of creator and narrator Rod Serling's clenched, yet mellifluous delivery evokes images from favorite episodes.

Such as . . .

"The Odyssey of Flight 33." A commercial airliner ends up in prehistoric times.

"It's a Good Life." A little boy maintains telepathic power over his family and town.

"Night of the Meek." A department store Santa finds himself holding a bag that dispenses an endless supply of presents.

"The Eye of the Beholder." A young woman lying in a hospital with her face bandaged hopes that an operation will cure her disfigurement.

WALKING DISTANCE

Sometimes as little as one line of dialogue or one camera shot evokes choice stories.

"It's... it's a cookbook!" Here are the climactic words from "To Serve Man," about extraterrestrials that come to our planet and cure all earthy ills, but with an ulterior motive.

A shot of the words "U.S. Air Force" on a spaceship: that's the inscription we finally see on an aircraft destroyed by an old woman in "The Invaders."

A counterman in a diner removes his cap to reveal a third eye, the conclusion to "Will the Real Martian Please Stand Up," about travelers at a rest stop who fear that one of them is an alien.

The list runs on and on.

As these descriptions suggest, the program's scripts varied widely in tone and subject, but over the years that *The Twilight Zone* flourished (1959–64), certain plot elements naturally recurred. Given its spirit of science fiction and fantasy, many stories involved space travel, both to and from Earth. Several scripts were set in the Old West, quite a few others in the midst of war, and even more in America of the near future or in some nameless distant society. Many, though, had contemporary settings and featured characters who discovered that their seemingly ordered lives were vulnerable to unnerving turmoil.

The effects of such chaos ranged from terrifying to wistful to ironic. Yet no matter the contents of an individual show, virtually all the stories suggested, directly or obliquely, greater significance. Indeed, many of those set in exotic environments dramatized issues that were prominent when the program ran on network television. Among these were the brutal effects of ignorance and bigotry, the pervasive suffering in war, the dangers of political paranoia, and the uncertain consequences of scientific exploration. But most scripts also encompassed more universal qualities: vanity and wisdom, cruelty and forgiveness, foolishness and understanding. Thus like all great drama, *The Twilight Zone* both reflected and transcended its time.

As such, the legacy of the program is boundless. Obvious and immediate successors included televisions shows like *The Outer Limits* and George Romero's *Tales from the Darkside*. To those we should add *Star Trek*, *Babylon 5*, and *Deep Space Nine*. Or, more recently, *Buffy the Vampire Slayer*, *Charmed*, and *The Walking Dead*.

Stephen King has commented movingly about the influence of *The Twilight Zone* on his output. So have such disparate figures as Rosanne Barr and David Chase, creator of *The Sopranos*.

Consider Stanley Kubrick's *2001: A Space Odyssey*, The *Star Wars* saga, and The Indiana Jones series. What about *Logan's Run*, based on a story by one of Serling's collaborators, George Clayton Johnson? Or *I am Legend* by another *Twilight Zone* writing mainstay, Charles Beaumont?

Think about the oeuvre of David Lynch, including films like *Eraserhead*, *Blue Velvet*, and *Mulholland Drive* and the television series *Twin Peaks*. What about M. Night Shayamalan ("*The Sixth Sense*")? Doesn't the line "I see dead people" belong in an episode of *The Twilight Zone*?

Don't forget television's The *X Files* and *Lost*. Or such anomalous movies as *Picnic at Hanging Rock* and *The Truman Show*. Or recent end-of-the-world scenarios like *Deep Impact* or *Melancholia*.

So many works may be traced back to one series.

Perhaps inevitably, the show invited parody. One of the earliest examples was a 1963 episode of *The Dick Van Dyke Show*, "It May Look Like a Walnut," about Rob Petrie's imagining an invasion of beings from the planet "Twylo." We should not be surprised to learn that writer and producer Carl Reiner proclaimed himself an unabashed fan of *The Twilight Zone* (Waldron 201).

Credit for the quality of the original series belonged not only to the writers but also to the hundreds of actors involved. Many were character players familiar from the dozens of weekly series shot in Hollywood during that time. Yet the roster also included distinguished veterans like Buster Keaton, Gladys Cooper, Ed Wynn, and Burgess Meredith, as well as newcomers who would eventually achieve eminence, among them Robert Redford, Charles Bronson, Anne Francis, Burt Reynolds, Leonard Nimoy, Robert Duvall, Don Rickles, and Carol Burnett. Again, every viewer has favorite performances, and to single out one is unfair. Nevertheless, in the spirit of this book and essay, I confess that I always return to Gig Young's portrayal of Martin Sloan in "Walking Distance." I cannot imagine any actor doing that part more effectively.

Ultimately, though, the success of the show rested on the writing. As indicated above, George Clayton Johnson and Charles Beaumont were regular contributors, as were Richard Matheson and Earl Hamner Jr., later the creator of *The Waltons*. But the guiding spirit was that of Rod Serling himself, who not only wrote dozens of scripts, but whose vision and humanity shone through every episode.

This observation returns us to "Walking Distance," for as much as any show in the series it reflects preoccupations that obsessed Serling throughout his adult life. To understand why, we must consider the arc of that life.

He was born on Christmas Day in 1924 in Syracuse, NY, but the family soon moved to nearby Binghamton, where young Rod enjoyed what might be judged an idyllic upbringing. All evidence suggests that at school he was a popular extrovert, while at home he enjoyed a healthy creative life with his brother, seven years Rod's senior. The two devoured pulp magazines like *Amazing Stories* and *Weird Tales*, and also enjoyed recreating scenes from movies they saw.

This happy period ended on the day Serling graduated from high school and entered World War II as a paratrooper. While in basic training he boxed successfully, then served in the Pacific, where he was wounded severely. Yet his suffering was not only physical; he would thereafter be haunted by the horrors he had witnessed. He also became immersed in two subjects that would dominate his creative output: a loathing for human cruelty and intolerance in whatever form he found it, and an ancillary fascination with boxing. During his time in the Philippines, he suffered more anguish when his father died of a heart attack, and the comfortable world Rod had known as a child was shattered. All these experiences created a sense of outrage within him that needed to find an outlet. As Serling later noted, ". . . I was bitter about everything and at loose ends when I got out of the service. I think I turned to writing to get it off my chest" (Zicree 5).

After completing work at Antioch College, he pursued a career in radio, but found himself frustrated by the narrowness of opportunity. Therefore he turned to the numerous live dramas that were then the staple of network television. He initially received some forty rejections, but between 1951 and 1955 dozens of his scripts were produced. His breakthrough was "Patterns," a highly praised drama about the moral dimensions of corporate infighting. This show was followed by one of the acknowledged gems of the era: the *Playhouse 90* production of *Requiem for a Heavyweight*, the single work of which Serling was always proudest. It also assured that his name would be included among those dramatists forever linked with the "Golden Age" of television, including Paddy Chayevsky, Reginald Rose, Horton Foote, Robert Alan Arthur, and Gore Vidal.

By the late 1950's, however, live anthology television had faded and been replaced by filmed shows that earned far greater profit from replay. Even more discouraging to Serling personally were his endless battles with censors and sponsors fearful of offending any segment of the viewership. Indeed, the logistics of trying to offer sustained quality while battling executive interference left him infuriated: "It is difficult to produce a television show that is both incisive and probing when every twelve minutes one is interrupted by twelve dancing rabbits singing about toilet paper" (Anton). But Serling understood the realities of his profession. Again in his own words: "The sponsor is king in television. And he always will be. It's a fact of life we must live with" (Grams 18).

Therefore he turned to creating his own series, and after extensive negotiations and sample scripts, *The Twilight Zone* premiered to immediate critical acclaim. It would never garner massive ratings, but it would always sustain a loyal audience for which Serling wrote an extraordinary ninety-two out of one hundred fifty-six episodes.

One of the first broadcast (on October 30, 1959) was "Walking Distance."

Not surprisingly, it met resistance from network personnel, who could not grasp that the fantasy elements coalesced into a workable story, but eventually the authorities relented. The entire budget for the show was less than $75,000, as outlined in *"The Twilight Zone": Unlocking the Door to a Television Classic* by Martin Grams, Jr. That total included $5000 for star Gig Young and $1250 for director Robert Stevens, paltry sums in light of present-day costs. Another notable contribution was the music by Bernard Hermann, whose other work includes scores for *Citizen Kane*, many science fiction classics of the 50s and 60s, and several films for Alfred Hitchcock, including *Psycho* and *Vertigo*.

A version of the script appeared in the first issue of *The Twilight Zone* magazine, which was published in the early 1980s, but an even earlier form has recently been printed in Volume 2 of *As Timeless as Infinity: The Complete "Twilight Zone" Scripts of Rod Serling*. The points of variance between this draft and the broadcast version are striking, and in the upcoming analysis I'll consider some.

Both versions begin with the familiar opening: the archetypal words, pictures, and music, and Serling's voice inviting us into "The Twilight Zone." The camera then pans down on a small gas station. The framing of the shot suggests the painting *Gas* by Edward Hopper, in which a filling station also sits against a country background. Even though the Hopper work features washed-out colors, while the program is in black-and-white, both evoke desolation.

WALKING DISTANCE

The silence is interrupted by a foreign car speeding with its top down, then noisily stopping amid a cloud of dust. The driver is young, good-looking, and dressed in a dark suit and tie, so we assume that he is successful. (In retrospect, the actor playing the driver, Gig Young, looks not unlike Rod Serling.) As the driver jams on the breaks, impatiently honks the horn, and brushes off his dusty clothes, we sense that whatever his social status, this man is unhappy. As he repeatedly sounds his horn, ending with one steady blare, the attendant remains calm: "Whenever you're finished, mister." The driver's answer is edgy: "How about some service?" To which the attendant maintains civility: "How about some quiet?" At this rebuff, the driver apologizes and requests a full tank, then smooths his hair. Meanwhile we forgive his rudeness and wonder about the reasons for his exasperation.

In the published draft of this script, the opening scene is more elaborate, as the driver fusses with a cigarette machine, then squabbles over lost change with the attendant, who seems bitter about his own life: "I see you guys from the city every week end . . . Ninety miles an hour—and just takin' a ride." That such lines were cut reaffirms a fundamental truth of dramatic writing: less is often more.

Then we hear the narrator's voice: "Martin Sloan, age 36." Which was almost exactly Serling's age at the time. Curiously, in the published script, Martin is described as "thirty-nine."

"Occupation: vice-president, ad agency, in charge of media." We need not hear more. We immediately picture Sloan sitting around a table surrounded by faceless men dressed exactly as he is, all bickering over a commercial for soap or cereal.

"This is not just a Sunday drive for Martin Sloan. He perhaps doesn't know it at the time . . . but it's an exodus." We note the Biblical connotations of "exodus."

"Somewhere up the road he's looking for sanity. (Pause) And somewhere up the road—he'll find something else."

We learn nothing further about Martin. We have no idea whether he has a wife, children, or, indeed, any relatives. We know nothing of his friends. Yet we care about him. Young presents a demeanor deserving sympathy, and the narration offers a forgiving tone. Thus we want this man to find whatever solace he seeks.

After the commercial break, the scene resumes with Martin's hair now miraculously combed. The attendant asks "Oil and lube job—is that what you want?" The original version has more dickering, again to no particular end. Martin agrees, then offers his own question: "That's Homewood up ahead, isn't it?" followed by "Grew up there, as a matter of fact. I haven't been back in twenty, twenty-five years."

Critics have disparaged the vagueness of this moment. Would a man start driving without any idea where he's going? Would he be so unaware that he has reached his home town? And because he later reveals that he attended school here until "third year high," wouldn't he know exactly how long since he left? Finally, at such a moment, why would he ask for an "oil change and lube job"?

Let's consider each objection.

I myself have started drives without any destination in mind. I've also revisited places I'd not seen for decades and managed to lose my way. Yet under either circumstance, I'm always aware of my vicinity, and Martin seems befuddled about even that. Possibly he's so desperate as to be literally lost. As for the time frame, Serling could simply have written "twenty years," clarifying that Martin was a junior in high school, roughly sixteen years old, when his family left Homewood. No doubt Serling was attempting to emphasize Martin's disorientation, but the uncertainty is so easily remedied that Serling may simply have been careless. Later Martin says that the time gap is precisely twenty years. As for Martin's request for an oil change and lube job, it's a plot device to start him walking, but also suggests that once out of New York, he has time to complete neglected chores.

He then reflects on the anxiety that inspired this drive: "I had to get out of New York. One more board meeting, phone call, report, problem—." Although the original draft contains further detail, we don't need it. Nor would we appreciate Martin's analysis of his reason for taking this journey, a line found only in the early script: "Going back to the womb, I guess you call it." Rather we easily imagine Martin back in New York, frantic among a slew of irritating messages and arguments. We can also picture Serling himself attempting desperately to balance demands from the economic powers he has to satisfy with his own artistic integrity. In sum, Martin is immediately identifiable, and as he begins his walk to "Homewood" (perhaps the symbolism is a bit heavy), we want to journey with him. By the way, the sign over the station identifies the owner as "Ralph W. Nelson," an inside joke, for that name belonged to the production manager for *The Twilight Zone*.

The most interesting touch, however, is Martin's reflection in the mirror of the cigarette machine. As the camera moves toward it, we see his image stride off, but we follow the camera right into the mirror, then seconds later observe it pull away from another mirror inside the Homewood drugstore. What is the significance of these shots? We can't be certain. We also never pass through the town of Homewood, but simply find ourselves in this establishment. Thus the question of what is real cannot be answered. Instead we are caught within what the show's opening tag famously called the "dimension of imagination."

Martin greets the counterman (Byron Foulger), a gentle figure whom Martin seems to recognize. The man demurs: "I got that kinda face." But what occupies Martin more is the thought of a chocolate ice cream soda with three scoops, and all for a dime. He adds that he used to spend hours at this fountain, although no one is sitting there right now. All seems normal and believable. The first unnerving moment occurs after Martin downs his chocolate soda and again grows nostalgic: "I'd almost expect Mr. Wilson to be sitting in the stock room and sleeping, just the way he always did before he died." The counterman looks quizzical, but before he responds, Martin pays for the ten-cent treat. The counterman is shocked: "That's a buck." But Martin does not care, and for the first time he seems happy. He jumps up, spins a few of the wooden counter seats, and bounds out the door. The counterman watches him, checks a container behind the fountain, and trudges up the stairs to the store room, where an old man snoozes. "Mr. Wilson?" the counterman asks. We wonder if we heard correctly. "Yup, Charlie?" answers the old man. Charlie's answer confirms our confusion: "We're gonna need some more chocolate sauce, Mr. Wilson."

What an elegant moment. It is quiet, but disquieting. We are apparently in the past, but we have no idea how we arrived. We are floating in some timeless place, and whether everything that has just occurred lies in either Martin's memory or his imagination is uncertain.

Before leaving this scene, we should observe that in the original typed version, Martin, still in the drugstore, sees a boy and a girl get into a 1933 or 1934 roadster, then pull away. Martin is taken aback, and is further disoriented upon meeting Mrs. Denton, who apparently knew him as a boy. When Martin identifies himself, then comments to the counterman how well she looks, we realize something is wrong. Yet all this information will later be clarified more economically, so this material, too, was deservedly excised.

Next we move to the streets of Homewood. Serling once recalled walking on a set at M-G-M and feeling how much it reminded him of

Binghamton. That incident, he explained, became the inspiration for "Walking Distance." He also often noted that he used to visit his hometown, especially a place called "Recreation Park," which had a merry-go-round much like the one in this script (Grams 83).

As Martin strolls the street, which years earlier was used for the film *Meet Me in St. Louis*, he recalls the occupants of each house, including "Dr. Bradbury," a tribute to the great writer Ray Bradbury. Although two of Bradbury's protégés, Matheson and Beaumont, became regular contributors to the series, only one of Bradbury's stories, "I Sing the Body Electric," was used, and Bradbury apparently remained bitter over what he viewed as a slight by Serling, whom he once considered a friend.

Suddenly Martin comes across a little boy shooting marbles. He is played by Ronnie Howard (as he is listed in the credits), who would soon achieve fame as Opie on *The Andy Griffith Show*, later as a teenager on *Happy Days*, and then as the eminent director of numerous major films, including *Cocoon*, *Apollo 13*, and *A Beautiful Mind*. Here Martin sits on the curb next to the boy and recalls when he, too, happily played with marbles. Young Howard struggles with his lines, especially after Martin points to the big white house where he used to live. The boy's response is barely audible: "The Sloan House?" But when Martin claims to be *the* Martin Sloan, the boy's panic is believable: "You're not Marty Sloan. I know Marty Sloan, and you're not him!" As Martin pulls out his wallet to provide proof, the boy peers curiously, then runs off, one more unsettling moment.

In the original script, this encounter is followed by a cameo featuring the little boy's father, Mr. Wilcox, then by Martin's knocking at the door of "the Sloan house." In the broadcast, however, the character of Mr. Wilcox has been cut, and Martin instead goes directly to the park, where he encounters a mother pushing a stroller and chasing her young son, who at that moment climbs a tree. Martin feels so at ease that he urges the boy to come down, a gesture that may strike us today as odd, for we view such invasive behavior from strangers as suspicious. But the vision here is of Martin's town the way he remembers it, where he feels "home," so we should accept his participation as benign.

Martin then chats with the woman about the delights around them: "the cotton candy, the ice cream, and the band concerts." In Martin's words, "Nothing is quite as good as summer and being a kid." Again, we might cynically reflect on the nature of summer in crowded cities or desolate plains, where no one escapes the scorching heat. But once more we realize that the vision here is of Martin's (and Serling's) idealized past, and as such it is free from intrusions of realism.

Yet even this fantasy cannot endure, for when Martin nears the merry go-round into which, as he tells the woman, he once carved his name, he sees a boy enacting the identical ritual. Suddenly nostalgia turns into terror, for Martin realizes the boy is himself: "Martin Sloan? *You're Martin Sloan?*" At first the boy assumes that he will be punished for vandalism: "Lots of kids carve their names here. Honest!" But Martin has different concerns: "You *are* Martin Sloan . . . That's the way I looked." This accusation sends the boy scurrying, and Martin races after him.

In the broadcast version, the scene moves back the Sloan house. In the published script, however, Martin stops and identifies himself to the woman with whom he just spoke. Then he explains: "I don't want to hurt him . . . I was going to tell him what would happen to him . . . If it's a dream . . . I suppose I'll wake up . . . But I don't want it to be a dream . . . I don't want time to pass now." With every confessional sentence, the script *tells* rather than *shows*, and although the scene has additional detail, the impact is diminished. Indeed, the amorphousness of these moments helps give this episode its timelessness. After all, Martin Sloan is compelling not because of the particulars of his life. Rather at this juncture he's all of us, or perhaps I should say that all of us identify with him. Thus we don't need him to articulate either what we ourselves feel or what we might feel in similar circumstances. The premise carries us along.

The scene in the park is followed by the encounter that the last few minutes have led us to expect. Martin walks to the front door of his old house and rings the bell, which is answered by the man he recognizes as his father. In the original script Martin mumbles "Dad," but in the televised version he calls his father "Pop." The distinction is subtle but significant, for "Pop" is more playful. Martin then hears his mother's voice: "Who is it, Robert?" Now his curiosity grows stronger: "Mom! Is that Mom!?" When both parents are framed in the shot, they stand behind the screen door that creates a filmy haze, as if the two figures exist on another plane of existence. Now Martin's wonder turns into desperation: "Mom, don't you know me? It's Martin!" But she doesn't recognize him, and at once Martin's helplessness becomes a pleading anger, beautifully enacted by Young: "Don't you know your own son?"

To Martin's despair, and ours, his parents do not acknowledge him. Indeed, his mother accuses him of being a "lunatic," after which his father shuts the door in Martin's face. Meanwhile Hermann's music echoes the torment inside Martin, who walks away in confusion, only to be greeted by a young man standing next to an automobile. For a moment Martin comes out of himself to acknowledge that he hasn't seen a car with a rumble seat in years. The published script, by the way, does not have this new character. Instead the car stands in the street, with a sign proclaiming it to be a "1934 roadster." The young man, however, is a more dramatic presence: "Where you been, Mister? Siberia? Pop just brought me this. First new car I've ever owned. Right out of Detroit yesterday morning." We suspect that the mention of the boy's father increases Martin's pain. This claim is followed by Martin's bemused response: "Brand new 1934 roadster. Right out of Detroit?" The young man never mentions the date, so this line is a remnant of the early version, but more importantly it manifests Martin's disorientation. We might add that although Martin seems shocked to see this particular vehicle, he has been walking the streets of the town for some time. Would he not have seen other older cars? And would not his own 1960s apparel have set him apart and aroused his curiosity, as well as that of others? Again, such inconsistencies do not detract from the tone of the piece. Rather they reinforce it.

After the commercial break, the episode resumes with a rare Serling narration in the middle:

> A man can think a lot of thoughts and walk a lot of pavements between afternoon and night. And to a man like Martin Sloan, to whom memory has suddenly become reality, a resolve can become as clearly and inexorably as stars of a night. Martin Sloan is now back in time. And his resolve is now to put in a claim to the past.

This transition leads to Martin's second confrontations with his father.

It begins with Martin's fingering objects from his youth: a baseball glove and the bell on his bicycle. This activity is interrupted by his father, Robert, whose attitude is one of curiosity, not anger: "Back again, huh?" Seemingly soothed by his father's cordiality, Martin speaks calmly: "I had to come back, Pop. This is my house." His father (played with great compassion by Frank Overton) answers gently: "Who are you? What do you want here?" Now Martin grows more unnerved: ""I just want to rest. I want to stop running." What touches us is how Robert sympathizes with this intruder. "I don't want to hurt you," he says, "and I don't want you to get into any trouble, either. But if you don't get out of here, there *will be* trouble." The speech is changed from the original script, which reads: "But you better get out of here or there *will be* trouble." The first version communicates danger; the broadcast version offers comfort.

The tranquility, however, breaks when we hear Martin's mother: "Who are you talking to, Rob—" Here Martin loses control and rushes to his mother (played by the familiar character actress Irene Tedrow), grabs her arms, and tries to make her see the truth:

> You've got a son named Martin, haven't you? He goes to Emerson Public School. The month of August he spends at his aunt's farm near Buffalo. And a couple of summers you've gone to Saratoga Lake. Once I had a sister. She died when she was a year old.

The memories are ordinary, but they are vivid, and that quality matters most. Martin might be any of us.

The climactic moments occur when his mother demands to know "Where's Martin?" to which Martin insists "*I'm Martin*! You've got to believe me!" Gig Young does not shout these lines, but the urgency in his voice communicates both fury and love. He needs her to understand, but he is unable to make her do so. In the printed text, he tries to furnish more evidence, but again the additional material does not help, because we already understand that his parents don't recognize him. In the actual show, on the other hand, Martin takes out his wallet and demands that she look at his credit cards and other identification, but instead she slaps his face. The gesture shocks both Martin and us.

Here the script and the broadcast diverge yet again. In the text Martin stares, then slowly wends his way from the house. In the broadcast, however, the calliope music immediately sounds, luring Martin back to the park. In the written version, the energy of the moment droops, but in the program it intensifies, as Martin runs past trees while the music pounds. Moreover, in the script when he reaches the park, virtually all action stops as Martin listens, waits, and sinks to the ground, then finally grows aware of the music, sees his younger self, and chases him through the park to confront a ticket taker. All these actions bog us down. In the telecast, however, the shot of Martin running faster and faster cuts to young Martin riding the merry-go-round, and thus the tension remains unabated.

Martin then jumps on the carousel and darts after his younger self, shouting his name. At the sight of the stranger, though, young Martin bounds off his horse and runs between the steeds on the merry-go-round. The pursuit grows more hectic until young Martin falls into the machinery and screams, "My leg, my leg!" In the next instant, the older Martin

The Twilight Zone

clutches his own leg and cries out. Quickly a mechanic stops the carousel, and young Martin is carried to safety. Meanwhile the older Martin walks lifelessly among the other children. Most stare blankly, and we again find ourselves caught between memory, reality, and fantasy. Since Martin has just hurt his leg, how can he walk so easily? Why does no one speak to him? In fact, the only voice we hear is that of Martin himself: "I only wanted to tell you that this is a wonderful time for you . . . Don't let any of it go by without enjoying it . . . That's all I wanted to tell you. God help me." And the scene fades out.

After a succession of shots showing the merry-go-round from different angles, confirming the bizarre world to which we have been transported, we see Martin sitting on the edge. In the script, one leg extends stiffly in front of him, but in the broadcast he shows no effects of the accident. Earlier he winced in agony, but now he has recovered. Thus once again viewers are stranded in a dramatic limbo between reality and . . . something else, an appropriate state for experiencing this show.

Martin's reverie is broken by the voice of his father, Robert: "I thought you'd want to know: the boy will be all right. The doctor says he may limp some, but he'll be all right." Martin repeats the image he had just invoked: "I thank God for that." Robert then hands Martin the wallet he dropped at the house: "It tells a great many things about you." Here his father acknowledges the date on Martin's driver's license, 1960, as well as Martin's identity, to which Martin replies, "Then you know, Pop." As the camera puts them in a two-shot, we realize that they could indeed be father and son. When Martin cannot explain how he has come here, Robert grounds their conversation: "But you know other things, don't you?" To which Martin nods. In the original script, the conversation is extended. In the broadcast version, however, Robert moves to the crucial sentiment: "You have to leave here. There's no room for you . . ." When Martin accepts that statement, but cannot understand why, Robert articulates the most painful truth of all: "I guess we only get once chance. Maybe there's only one summer to a customer." The juxtaposition of a traditional expression of salesmanship with an image of mortality is elegant.

Robert then asks: "Is it so bad—where you're from?" And in Martin's answer we hear Serling's voice: "I thought so . . . I've been living at a dead run . . . I had to stop and breathe and close my eyes and smell and listen." For those who know of Serling's frenzied existence, his endless battles with superiors, his relentless sessions at the typewriter, and his four-to-five cigarette packs day, the phrase "life at a dead run" encapsulates Serling's own life, which would be cut off at age fifty.

The scene ends with Robert's counsel: "You've been looking behind you, Martin. Try looking ahead." Martin's answer, however, is half-hearted: "Maybe. Goodbye, Pop." Robert's next and last line is inevitable but still wrenching: "Good-bye . . . son." Then the merry-go-round starts to revolve, and Martin steps up and grabs hold. Like a rat racing on a wheel in a cage, he feels the relentless circle of his life resume.

The final juxtaposition brings us back to 1959, where inside the drugstore teenagers now cluster. We also note, as the published script suggests, "the blare of rock-n-roll." To twenty-first-century ears, the music sounds harmless, almost old-fashioned, but when the script was first broadcast, the rhythm and instrumentation were jarring. Moreover, the new soda jerk is now a young man, sprightly and congenial, but his manner nevertheless contrasts with that of the older gentleman who earlier ran the store. Martin inquires about an ice cream soda with three scoops, but upon learning that it now costs thirty-five cents, withdraws his request. He also asks about Mr. Wilson, but is told that "he died about fifteen, twenty years ago." When Martin steps off his old perch, he lurches awkwardly, then comments: "These stools weren't meant for bum legs, were they?" The soda jerk asks, "Hey, got that during the war?" To which Martin replies: "No, no. As a matter of fact I got it falling off a merry-go-round when I was a kid. Freak thing." He seems to have forgotten the circumstances, another instance where reality and memory stand at odds.

The counterman observes that the merry-go-round was torn down a few years ago, then adds: "A little late for you." Martin agrees: "Very late. Very late for me." In other words, we have no happy ending. If we anticipated that the encounter with his father would change Martin for the better, perhaps making him more optimistic, we were wrong. Earlier he was angry. Now he seems resigned.

The epilogue to this show is the most beautiful passage Serling ever wrote. As Martin returns to the gas station (walking with a noticeably stiff leg), Serling's voice speaks over Bernard Hermann's ethereal chords:

> Martin Sloan, age thirty-six. Vice-president in charge of media. Successful in most things—but not in the one effort that all men try at some time in their lives—trying to go home again.

> And also like all men perhaps there'll be an occasion ... maybe a summer night some time ... when he'll look up from what he's doing and listen to the distant music of a calliope—and hear the voices and the laughter of the people and the places of his past. And perhaps across his mind there'll flit a little errant wish ... that a man might not have to become old—never outgrow the parks and the merry-go-rounds of his youth.
>
> And he'll smile then, too, because he'll know it is just an errant wish. Some wisp of memory not too important really. Some laughing ghosts that cross a man's mind ... that are a part of *The Twilight Zone*.

I don't remember my initial viewing of this program, which would have first run when I was eleven, but I have watched it dozens of time since, and it affects me each time. I even show it to my college classes, and my impression is that this story touches something within my students as well. They seem especially sensitive to the theme of transience, that no matter our ambitions or accomplishments, life passes with terrifying quickness, and disappointment and frustration are an inevitable part of our struggle. The show also dramatizes our fundamental loneliness. Not only does mortality loom over us; so does the recognition that in the end we face it alone.

At the risk of pretension, I must note that "Walking Distance" reminds me of what I believe is the most moving one-act stage play ever written: Samuel Beckett's *Krapp's Last Tape*. In this work set in the future, a solitary old man listens to a recording he made thirty years before, when he was listening to an even earlier tape of his own voice. As he hears himself ruminate on hope, love, and loss, the evanescence and futility of existence torments him as acutely as it does Martin Sloan.

It also tormented Rod Serling, who dramatized this theme in numerous episodes. In "The Sixteen-Millimeter Shrine," telecast for the first time a week before "Walking Distance," an actress from the early days of movies (Ida Lupino) watches her old films while she remains insulated from the world around her. She wants so much to preserve her youth that she is actually transported into one of her movies. In "A Stop at Willoughby," harried businessman Gart Williams (James Daly) dreams during his commuter ride home that he has reverted to the 1880s and to summer in the pastoral town of Willoughby. After the dream recurs, he steps off the train to join the welcoming citizens, but when the winter of reality returns, the body of Mr. Williams is borne away in an ambulance marked "Willoughby & Sons, Funeral Home." And in "The Trouble With Templeton," written by E. Jack

WALKING DISTANCE

Neuman, aging actor Booth Templeton, (Brian Aherne) longs for earlier, simpler days, but when he finds himself back in 1927 and encounters the ghosts of his wife and friends, they reject him. Ultimately he is restored to the present, but imbued with a desire to live fully in the moment. Of all Serling's time-travel stories, this one may be the most positive.

"Walking Distance," however, remains the most potent. To be sure, it has been the subject of controversy. Ray Bradbury, who never did reconcile with Serling, insisted that the use of a merry-go-round demonstrated how the show actually originated in his own short story "The Black Ferris." In addition, Gore Vidal, who knew Serling from their days in live television, claimed that "Walking Distance" was plagiarized from his story "A Moment of Green Laurel," in which a man visiting his home town of Washington D.C. encounters what seems to be a young version of himself. But in the article "The Many Fathers of Martin Sloan," Christopher Conlon explores how despite surface similarities with these other efforts, the Serling teleplay is unique. First, the Bradbury piece, aside from that one symbol, has almost nothing in common with "Walking Distance," while in Vidal's story the meeting between man and boy is virtually instantaneous and goes no further. Furthermore, as Conlon notes, the theme of time travel paradoxes had been used often before.

We have acknowledged the wonderful performance by Gig Young as Martin Sloan, but when seen in the light of Young's own life it becomes more poignant. The actor was born Byron Barr in 1913, then took his stage name from that of his character in the 1942 film *The Gay Sisters*. He enjoyed a substantial career, often as the charming, if ironic, partner to the leading players. He earned Academy Award nominations for his work in *Come Fill the Cup* and as the psychiatrist who counsels Clark Gable in *Teacher's Pet*, and finally won Best Supporting Actor in 1972 as the cynical dance marathon promoter in *They Shoot Horses, Don't They?* By then, however, Young was already a heavy drinker, and the award only exacerbated his sense of inadequacy.

His personal life was also chaotic. He married five times, and his third wife was actress Elizabeth Montgomery, later the star of *Bewitched*, who divorced him because of his alcoholism. In 1978, at age sixty-four, he married thirty-one-year-old Kim Schmidt, but three weeks later the two were found dead in their Manhattan home. The official report stated that Young had shot his wife, then himself.

The Twilight Zone

To view an artist's work through the prism of that person's life is risky. Nevertheless, when we watch "Walking Distance" with knowledge of the demons that Young endured, we can only speculate how much of Martin Sloan's pain emerged from the actor's own suffering.

My enthusiasm for "Walking Distance" does not diminish my appreciation for other episodes of *The Twilight Zone*, of which I'll mention two that reflect different aspects of Rod Serling's work. One is "The Monsters are Due on Maple Street," originally broadcast March 4, 1960. The premise is simple. When all the machines and utilities on Maple Street suddenly stop, a neighborhood boy proposes that invaders from space have infiltrated the population, and within moments the citizens turn on one another in panic. The show is a skillful reflection of the political hysteria that beset the 1950s, and numerous speeches resound with chilling precision, such as: "You best watch who you're seen with, Steve! Until we get all this straightened out, you ain't exactly above suspicion yourself." This line and others evoke the destructive activities of HUAC, the blacklist that terrorized the entertainment industry, and the pervasive fear that dominated the era of McCarthyism. At the end of this show, as the residents of Maple Street run riot, the camera pans upward to a pair of aliens who reflect how under such circumstances the inhabitants of Earth will "pick the most dangerous enemy they can find . . . and it's themselves." The closing narration reflects perhaps the most deeply held of all Serling's convictions:

> The tools of conquest do not necessarily come with bombs explosions and fallout. There are weapons that are simply thoughts, attitudes, prejudices—to be found only in the minds of men. For the record, prejudices can kill, and suspicions can destroy, and a thoughtless frightened search for a scapegoat has a fallout all its own for the children . . . and the children yet unborn. And the pit of it is . . . that these things cannot be confined to . . . *The Twilight Zone*.

The other script I'll mention is less celebrated, but remains a favorite of mine because it represents one of the rare light moments in the series. "A World of His Own" was written by Richard Matheson, and features Keenan Wynn as playwright Gregory West, who can conjure up human beings by describing them into a Dictaphone. When his wife, Victoria, objects to his creating another woman for companionship, West mournfully opens his wall safe and pulls out the tape on which, he claims, she is described. Victoria scoffs at this threat and throws the tape into the fire, but to her astonishment she disappears. Free at last, West summons up the gentle, loving woman he had previously envisioned.

The most delightful touch, however, is the ending, when Serling comes onscreen to wrap up the story: "We hope you enjoyed tonight's romantic story on *The Twilight Zone*. At the same time, we want you to realize that it was, of course, purely fictional. In real life, such ridiculous nonsense could never . . ." Here he is interrupted by the character West: "Rod. You shouldn't. You shouldn't have said such things, Rod. Like 'nonsense.' 'Ridiculous.'" West then goes to the safe to retrieve an envelope marked "Rod Serling" and tosses it into the fire. Serling sadly fades from view as his voice echoes: ". . . leaving Mr. Gregory West . . . in complete control in *The Twilight Zone*." The script is not only charming. It's a provocative commentary about the act of creation that gives a writer godlike power over the lives of characters. As a playwright, I find that concept irresistible.

The history of *The Twilight Zone* (the original series) was comparatively brief. From October 1959-September 1962, it ran in a half-hour format. In January 1963 the show was expanded to a full hour, but in the following fall the half-hour structure was restored. From May 1963-September 1964, some of those hour-long shows were rerun, and thereafter the series was revived fitfully. Without the guiding influence of Rod Serling, though, it withered.

As for Serling himself, after the series ended, he seemed to return to what years earlier he had called "loose ends." He created a show called *The Loner*, about a battle-weary Confederate soldier who was as displaced as Martin Sloan, but the series received uneven reviews and lasted barely one season. Serling did achieve success with his script for movie *Planet of the Apes*, but even this celebrated effort may be regarded as a retread of *The Twilight Zone*, for the conclusion, when Charlton Heston discovers that all along he has been on Earth, was borrowed from the episode "I Shot an Arrow in the Air."

Serling did return to television from 1970–73 with the series *Night Gallery*, but the experience was unhappy. Although he wrote a third of the scripts, he repeatedly clashed with producer Jack Laird, who emphasized terror and horror rather than enlightened and enlightening fantasy. One episode, however, warrants citation: "They're Tearing Down Tim Riley's Bar." It dramatizes the plight of businessman Randy Lane, who, after twenty-five years in the same job selling plastics, finds himself at a dead end. His wife died years ago, a passing for which Randy feels guilty, for he was too busy working to bring her to the hospital. Meanwhile a ruthless younger rival is pushing Randy aside, his boss barely acknowledges him, and Randy sees little point in going on. Today, on this anniversary, he is to receive a gold watch, but the gift is meaningless, especially when Randy knows that his favorite bar is about to be demolished. Here is where he came after returning home from World War II, and where he and his wife shared their happiest moments. When he visits the site, though, he peers in the window and sees the ghosts of his past.

The bond between this show and "Walking Distance" is obvious, but subtle differences are worth noting. One, Randy Lane is forty-eight years old, a decade older than Martin Sloan and virtually the same age as Serling when he wrote the teleplay. Two, we actually meet the business rival (Bert Convy) who embodies all the unseen forces that plague Martin Sloan. And three, even though Randy feels intense loneliness, he does have the support of Miss Alcott, played by Diane Baker, who speaks movingly about Randy in front of the office personnel. Thus the ending is more upbeat than that of "Walking Distance."

"They're Tearing Down Tim Riley's Bar" was nominated for an Emmy, and stands as Serling's last great piece. It may also be regarded as his own elegy. Over the next few years he taught at Ithaca College (near his hometown), made cameo appearances on shows like "Laugh-In," and performed commercial voiceovers, an ironic outlet for someone who spent many years in conflict with sponsors.

In a final interview before his death in 1975, Serling commented: "God know when I look back over thirty years of professional writing, I'm hard-pressed to come up with anything that's important" (Brevelle). The operative word, of course, is "important." Rod Serling helped bring American television to maturity, he expanded our view of the world, and he influenced innumerable artists after him. I believe that such accomplishments deserved to be judged "important."

I also believe that anyone who wants to appreciate Serling's greatness need only watch "Walking Distance."

II

The Phil Silvers Show (You'll Never Get Rich)

"The Court Martial"

and

McHale's Navy

"Dear Diary"

The first prime-time show that became requisite viewing for me was *The Phil Silvers Show*, originally titled *You'll Never Get Rich*. But like millions of other Americans, I never referred to the program by either title. Instead, from the start of its run in 1955 until the end in 1959, we all called the show simply "Bilko." Or maybe "Sergeant Bilko." And for the rest of his life, Phil Silvers would play some variation of the title character: a fast-talking, larcenous, yet ultimately likeable flimflam man.

The show was broadcast on Tuesday evenings at 8:00, 8:30, or 9:00, but whatever the specific time, "Bilko" was essential to my weekly routine, and I planned my evenings around it. Admittedly, I wasn't nearly as independent as that statement implies. When the series started, I was seven and allowed to watch only on the condition that I would go to bed immediately afterwards so as to be capable of functioning in school the next day.

The Phil Silvers Show and *McHale's Navy*

When "Bilko" ended, I was bereft of a certain outlet for amusement, but that void was filled in 1962, when another service comedy, *McHale's Navy*, hooked me after one viewing. What's more, I stayed hooked until it ended in 1966. It played Thursday evenings, first at 9:30, then at 8:30, but the slot didn't matter because by then I was in high school and somewhat of a free agent, at least in terms of bedtime.

The similarities between the two were plentiful. Both shows involved military units, one in the army, the other in the navy. Both outfits were run by mid-level officers who were, to say the least, fun-loving and disdainful of authority. And both officers reported to higher-ups determined to curtail the shenanigans in which these units indulged.

Bilko's motor pool platoon was stationed initially at Fort Baxter in Roseville, Kansas, then later in California. In each setting peacetime held sway, so Master Sergeant Ernest Bilko had opportunity to orchestrate a non-stop series of rackets designed to separate all personnel on the post from their money. He and Colonel Hall, played with endearing befuddlement by Paul Ford, were forever at odds, as Bilko talked his way from one scam to another, and the Colonel did his best to undermine him.

Quinton McHale, on the other hand, as played by Ernest Borgnine, commanded a PT-Boat during WWII in the Pacific, where members of his crew were conveniently stationed on their own island. From here they conducted dangerous patrols, but their isolated outpost also permitted them to sleep late, gamble, consort with women and natives, sell booze, and otherwise carouse free from the regulations endured by the rest of the sailors and nurses on the main base. Although the threat of combat was constant, the real opposition was the unit commander, Captain Binghamton, whose personal mission was not only to end the unmilitary activities of those he denigrated as "McHale's pirates," but to decimate the crew and send its members packing.

One more attribute that Bilko and McHale shared: both did their official jobs superbly.

Yet one other attribute that the shows shared: both struck me as riotously funny.

The programs had several creative personnel in common. Billy Sands, who played Private Paparelli on "Bilko," played Seaman Harrison "Tinker" Bell on "McHale's." Bob Hastings, who occasionally played an officious or sycophantic sergeant or lieutenant on "Bilko," was cast permanently as an officious and sycophantic lieutenant on "McHale's." And George Kennedy, who initially served as a consultant on "Bilko," then took a few walk-on parts, guest-starred several times on "McHale's" as "Big Frenchy," an amiable but unscrupulous rival of McHale's. A few years later, Kennedy won an Oscar as Best Supporting Actor for his performance in *Cool Hand Luke*.

Perhaps the most important link between the two shows was Edward J. Montagne, who after producing selected episodes of "Bilko" served as producer, then executive producer, for the entire run of "McHale's." Montagne's television career dated from the beginnings of the medium, but he had assisted and directed in movies as far back as the 1930s. He even worked (uncredited) with W.C. Fields on *The Bank Dick*, an experience that must have taught him something about the art of comedy, including the need for spritely pace and an emphasis on physical humor that both shows offered aplenty.

In one vital way, however, the programs were different.

"Bilko" revolved mostly around the man himself. As the majority of episode titles suggested, his machinations created many of the plot lines, and the rest of the base population responded to his schemes, virtually always aimed at acquiring money, e.g., Bilko has a new poker system, Bilko thinks he has a winning racehorse, Bilko finds a baseball prodigy. Sometimes Bilko simply wanted to avoid bivouac or a cold blast of winter. Once his plan was unleashed, though, all around him, including his platoon, his fellow sergeants, and the rest of the officers, scrambled to avoid being caught in the whirlwind. In that sense Bilko was the embodiment of a great American tradition: the trickster for whom the rest of the world is comprised of suckers primed to be fleeced.

On *McHale's Navy*, however, the title character, "Skipper" to his crew, was essentially the straight man. In 1955 Borgnine won an Academy Award for *Marty*, and during the mid-sixties was by far the most prestigious member of the cast. Indeed, in one episode Captain Binghamton taunts McHale about an actor who won an Academy Award: "You've never seen one of those, have you?" In another episode, when the crew is on shore leave, McHale and his executive officer, Ensign Parker, exchange this dialogue:

"What do you want to do, Chuck?"

"I don't know. Skip. What do you want to do?"

"I don't know."

The lines echo a memorable scene from *Marty*. Otherwise, however, McHale was a courageous, if rowdy, former merchant seaman who knew the islands of the South Pacific like the proverbial "back of his hand." Thus

The Phil Silvers Show and McHale's Navy

while McHale led combat missions and maintained his crew in fighting shape, the comic chores were handled by young Tim Conway as Ensign Parker, in what would prove a breakout role, and Joe Flynn as the Captain.

Before we consider those gentlemen, however, let's start with "Bilko" and that one-man tornado, Phil Silvers.

After beginning his career as a boy singer in the Gus Edwards Revue in the 1920s, he moved into vaudeville and burlesque. There he developed the manic style that would characterize him for the rest of his career (although offstage he was said to be quiet and introspective). With his bald pate and rimmed glasses, he appeared bookish, but he had a wide grin often accompanied by a dynamic greeting such as "How aaah yaaaah!?" or "Glad da see yaaah!" Either phrase confirmed that he was the most transparent of operators who had found a suitable pigeon.

When Silvers moved from burlesque to films, his career, largely in musicals, was steady but unremarkable. As he described his persona, "I always seemed to play the same part – Blinky, the hero's friend who in the last reel told Betty Grable that the guy really loved her" (Metz 129). Among his best movies were *Cover Girl* (1944) and *Summer Stock* (1950). Along the way he wrote the lyrics for "Nancy with the Laughing Face," a song about Frank Sinatra's daughter that became one of the singer's biggest hits.

Silvers' star began to rise with his performance of the title role in the Broadway show *Top Banana* (1952). He played Jerry Biffle, an ego-driven television comic based on Silvers' good friend Milton Berle, who at that time was the biggest star in the new medium and known to all as "Mr. Tuesday Night" or "Uncle Miltie." Biffle not only incorporated Silvers' limitless energy and capacity for patter, but allowed him to recreate routines he had honed for years in burlesque, and perform them with buddies from that era who were also in the show.

In 1954 the head of CBS saw Silvers emcee a White House Correspondents dinner, and was so taken with the performance that he suggested to Silvers that he and Nat Hiken, a veteran comedy writer from radio and television, should develop a half-hour format. The relationship between the two flourished, and the result was *You'll Never Get Rich*. Throughout their collaboration, Silvers' admiration for Hiken never diminished. In fact, upon accepting an Emmy for his performance as Bilko, Silvers gave full credit to "a genius, Nat Hiken." The name "Bilko," by the way, sounds like an extension of "bilk," but was actually taken from a minor league ballplayer Hiken admired named Steve Bilko, who once hit sixty-one home runs in a season. Hiken made his Bilko a sergeant so that he had chances to operate and a platoon to control, but was nonetheless subordinate to other officers.

The rest of the large "Bilko" company reflected Hiken's singular casting tastes (in one sitcom he paired comedienne Martha Raye with former middleweight champion Rocky Graziano), and in Bilko's platoon he created a marvelous hodgepodge, although in retrospect they seem a mite old for their parts. Herbie Faye, for instance, a burlesque veteran and a longstanding crony of Silvers, played Sam Fender. When the show began, Faye was fifty-five, but his character was still a private and the sole support of a wife and several children. Another regular was Jack Healy as Private Mullen. He was not a trained actor, but a former manager of the aforementioned Graziano.

The most unusual member of the platoon was Maurice Gosfield, who played the woebegone Private Duane Doberman. When he appeared at an open call, he was immediately cast as the company patsy. Congenitally sloppy, just like his character, and with little experience or discipline, Gosfield apparently irritated the highly professional Silvers, but nonetheless was enormously popular among viewers (Metz 129). One of the regular motifs of the show was that whenever Bilko needed a fall guy, Doberman was selected, even though he tried desperately to resist Bilko's summons: "Why me, Sarge? Why is it always me?"

Perhaps the most noteworthy casting decision rated hardly any attention at the time. Among the multitude of ethnic groups in Bilko's barracks, which included Gomez, Zimmerman, Kadowski, and Paparelli, one man was always African American. Moreover, whenever new recruits entered, we again saw at least one black man. Moreover, these soldiers were treated the same as everyone else, a remarkable occurrence in the 1950s. Silvers often related how years after "Bilko" ended, he was mugged in New York City by an unemployed black actor who suddenly recognized his victim, said "You're okay," and released Silvers.

Also worth mentioning is the presence of women in the series as officers and noncoms. Admittedly they didn't fight (no one else did, either), but they kept Fort Baxter running with whatever efficiency Bilko allowed. African American women were part of this contingent as well.

"Bilko" was taped at the DuMont Studios on 67th Street in New York City, above a delicatessen where the cast often gathered. Each show was presented almost as a straight play, but with three cameras. The sets were stark, with the feel of a real barracks, and the action always felt appropriately

The Phil Silvers Show and McHale's Navy

cramped. Each show was taped straight through; thus in virtually every episode actors fumble for lines or simply "go up." Paul Ford as Colonel Hall was especially prone to memory slips, so Silvers constantly cued him: "You were saying, sir, about the jeep . . ." Yet because of the Colonel's innate confusion, such scrambling never proved a distraction. Furthermore, given the pace at which Bilko/Silvers talked, and the number of words he had to articulate, "Bilko" scripts were particularly long. Silvers also regularly muttered asides, repetitions, or denials to whoever stood nearby, and words seemed to cascade out of him until someone, usually the Colonel, shouted "Bilko!" and thereby restored a measure of order and allowed the show to proceed.

Perhaps the most celebrated "Bilko" episode is "The Court Martial," also known as "The Case of Harry Speakup." The show is atypical in that Bilko is the reactor rather than the instigator, but the script not only provides Silvers with the opportunity to perform some glorious verbal pyrotechnics, but also offers a brilliant portrait of officialdom running amok. The script, written by Hiken, Coleman Jacoby, and Arnie Rosen, and directed by Al DeCaprio, was originally broadcast on March 6, 1956. Three years later, Silvers said of its premise, "When Nat Hiken suggested the idea, I flipped. Up to then we had a reasonable amount of plausibility in the show – and this seemed ridiculous. So I said to Nat, 'Make it plausible and we'll do it. And he made it plausible, awfully plausible. I tell you it's the funniest half-hour on television unconditionally" (philsilversshow.com). Nearly sixty years later, that judgment still warrants consideration.

The episode begins in the Colonel's office, where he announces to assembled officers that he hopes to show the General that Fort Baxter can process 300 new men within three hours, then induct them into the service. Except, of course, if there is "a monkey wrench thrown in . . ." At this warning, Bilko takes umbrage: "Really, sir, I—" But the Colonel cuts him off. Hall then promises that a successful effort will mean promotions, including one for himself. This guarantee inspires one of Bilko's characteristically impassioned overtures: "You'll be missed around here, sir." To capture the precise nature of Silvers' delivery of this and countless other fraudulent compliments is impossible, but I'll try. He started with vibrating tones that would fit a particularly bombastic member of the British theater, then enunciated every word with a hint of epicene precision. The manner was patently phony but irresistibly funny. It succeeded particularly well with the Colonel's wife (Hope Sansberry), whom Bilko continually pretended

WALKING DISTANCE

to mistake for someone's daughter, if not a model or an actress, only to be apparently shocked at the revelation of her identity: "Bless my soul! It's Mrs. Hall! Oh, they'll going to call you a cradle-robber, sir!"

At this juncture in the episode, Bilko begins to sing in his inimitable faux-operatic treble, a song that he favors from time to time: "Should auld acquaintance be forgot—" But the chorus is cut off by the Colonel, who warns that the General will also be inspecting barracks. Now Bilko becomes nervous: "The General is coming to my barracks for inspection? Sir, may I suggest—" But the Colonel has no choice: "It's too late to burn your barracks."

What an economic scene, in which not a word is wasted. Within a couple of minutes we have clearly delineated characters, a premise, and tension, so that even someone who has never seen the series can grasp its essence.

Back in the barracks, Bilko and his two corporals-in-crime, Barbella (Harvey Lembeck) and Henshaw (Allan Melvin), attempt to prepare for inspection, but suddenly Bilko spies the hangdog Doberman in the front row. Bilko has a solution: "Take care of the furnace room, Doberman." "In the middle of summer?" is the private's response. "You never know. The wind may shift" is Bilko's instantaneous reply, followed by the signature guttural command that Silvers invoked in every episode. It sounded something like "Heeyah, heeyah, har har, hun, two, hun, two." Sometimes it devolved into a simple roar, but letters and words cannot do justice to the ferocity that Silvers summoned to send subordinates scurrying and which became a Silvers' trademark.

When the new recruits enter, one drags a large sack. This recruit is Private Charlie Chapman, played by an actor with a familiar face and an entertaining story of his own. His name was Joey Faye (no relation to Herbie), and he was another of Silvers' cohorts from burlesque. Indeed, he was often called the greatest "second banana" in show business, and he famously boasted an endless assortment of sneezes. He even claimed to have originated two classic comedy routines: "Fluegel Street" and "Slowly I Turned." Still, after a lifetime of silliness, he insisted that his favorite performance was as Estragon in Samuel Beckett's *Waiting for Godot*.

Bilko orders Chapman to deposit his equipment in the furnace room. Chapman complies, but within seconds a monkey on skates emerges from the sack, then rolls through the barracks. Bilko cannot believe what he has seen, but Barbella asserts the reality of the situation: "Sarge, that wasn't

The Phil Silvers Show and McHale's Navy

Doberman. That was a monkey." Silvers laughs off this claim, but then sees that it is legitimate, so when the general enters and inspection begins, the men instinctively form a circle to hide the intruder (whose name turns out to be Zippo). The general inquires about such a peculiar formation, but Bilko offers a retort:

> "It's just an example of the vision of our commanding officer. We're in constant training becoming acquainted with military maneuvers of foreign nations . . . Surely the general recognizes the British Square . . . The Square that won over India, you know . . . I wish I had time to show the General the Armenian Oblong . . ."

The barrage of words leaves everyone at a loss. Nonetheless, the Colonel, long familiar with Bilko's antics, suspects trouble, but Bilko dissuades him: "A British cheer for the Colonel, men. Hip, hip—" Fortunately the recruits are swept up in his energy and respond appropriately, and a buffaloed Colonel Hall departs. Meanwhile Bilko orders his men to hide Zippo in the latrine, then looks to the heavens: "Why? Why?"

Two aspects of the previous scene are worth a moment's pause. One, as Joey Faye seems to lead the monkey, another fellow stands in the middle of the soldiers, next to Bilko and carrying Zippo. This new recruit is played by Lee Ecuyer, Zippo's real-life trainer. Throughout the episode, he follows Zippo and blends into the action so smoothly that we might not notice him, but in fact he keeps the monkey under control. In this scene, however, Zippo keeps grabbing for Bilko's cap, and given that this show is live, we wonder whether Zippo has been cued or if he is misbehaving on his own. Meanwhile Silvers turns with complete commitment to the monkey and orders him to desist. The laughter from the audience, unamplified as always, suggests they realize that Silvers is ad libbing in character, and the scene plays wonderfully. The writers even give Ecuyer a line. When Bilko tells the men to hide Zippo in the latrine, Ecuyer asks, "What's a latrine?"

Before Bilko and his men can get rid of Zippo, however, the intruder becomes caught up in the induction medical line. At this moment, we remember the Colonel's warning that a "monkey wrench" might be thrown in. Did the writers insert an intentional pun?

Meanwhile the bureaucratic machine races crazily. As one doctor asks for the monkey's medical history, to which Zippo naturally says nothing, another officer demands a response: "Hurry! Speak up!" And suddenly a new soldier, "Harry Speakup," joins the parade. We also observe that trainer Ecuyer follows under the name "Martin Ford."

WALKING DISTANCE

When Bilko learns that all his recruits have passed through that phase of enlistment, he gratefully assumes that the monkey has been removed, but suddenly he sees someone or something skate past him with a cigarette: "No smoking!" Bilko shouts, then realizes what has happened. He appeals to Captain Barker to stop the wave of inductees, but Barker does not believe him and orders Bilko to visit the Colonel. In the meantime, the dentist passes Harry with no problem ("Overdeveloped Canines. Extreme underbite"). The foot doctor can't quite fathom what he has witnessed and momentarily delays the onslaught, but Harry soon slips through, along with the omnipresent Martin Ford.

Even the psychiatrist proves no problem. While the doctor conducts his interview without even glancing at his subject, Zippo spins wildly on the table. Naturally the monkey passes, accepts the approved form, and skates off, followed by a soldier named "Bill Benson," but played, as the careful viewer notes, by Ecuyer. The last stop is the intelligence test, where Benson/Ford and the monkey sit next to each other. When one bright recruit finishes quickly, Bilko switches answer sheets, signs Zippo's name, and one more hurdle is passed.

All these procedures are conducted at warp speed. Meanwhile, as the military machine rolls on, the laughter from the studio audience is nonstop.

When examinations for the entire group conclude, the Colonel and his staff congratulate one another. Finally Bilko blurts out the truth, but before anyone can act on this news, we hear the enlistment oath being administered by the General. Bilko tries to evade blame, even for the Colonel: "It's nobody's fault, sir." But Hall is inconsolable: "They'll remember me as the man that opened the doors of the Army to the animal kingdom."

When the General is informed about his blunder, he is, of course, furious, and conceives what he assumes is a workable solution: "Throw him out for having subnormal intelligence." The problem? Because Bilko switched tests, "[Zippo] was the third highest in the group." Still, Bilko tries to bolster everyone's spirits: "He's a bright little monkey!" But everyone blames him anyway. The only answer is a court-martial, for which Bilko is appointed defense counsel. To save himself, he must save Zippo, and thus begins one of the most joyously preposterous scenes in television history.

With the Colonel's office arranged as a miniature courtroom (reminding us again that the show was filmed like a play), the General shouts for all red tape to be cut and for the trial to proceed. Bilko, of course, objects: "Sir, I'd like a postponement," but before he can supply details, Zippo is escorted in by an MP, played by the same actor who played Ford/Benson, Lee Ecuyer. Zippo then sits at a table next to Bilko, and while the other officers conduct proceedings, Bilko confers intensely with his client. The conversation is one-sided, but Bilko's performance is a classic example of what actors call staying "in the moment." While Bilko's silent words and gestures of reassurance absorb us, the first witness, Sergeant Siwicki (Harry Clark), the company cook, explains that Zippo bit him in a struggle over some bananas. Immediately Bilko objects once more, this time to the use of the derogatory word "monkey": "The defendant is a private in the United States Army . . ." Here the monkey bangs the table (whether on cue we cannot say), so Bilko, always maintaining character, affirms his client's frustration: "That's right! He is privileged to be addressed by his full rank . . . a rank that so many glorious men in the past have . . ." Finally, in the interests of expediency, the General agrees to the objection.

Then Bilko demands the right to cross-examine Siwicki, who admits that he could not understand the defendant's "chattering." Bilko, however, is unimpressed: "Did it ever occur to you, sir, that in his way he was trying to tell you that the bananas were his? And didn't it occur to you that as a private he is entitled to be fed by the United States Army?" When the general repeats the charge that "Private Speakup" actually bit a non-commissioned officer "maliciously," Bilko is shocked: "Maliciously, sir? Could he?" Again we are reminded that the program is live, as during an awkward pause right here, no one speaks until Silvers skips to his next cue and accuses Sergeant Siwicki of attacking Zippo. Now Bilko tries to have all charges dismissed, but suddenly the monkey jumps from his perch at the defendant's desk and bounces to the telephone. The action seems to catch Bilko (and Silvers) by surprise, but whether Zippo reacts spontaneously or not, Bilko's panicked response is priceless: "Just a minute, sir. I think he's calling for another lawyer!" As the brief exchange unfolds, the other actors onstage look away, as if fearful of exploding in laughter.

Presently Private Chapman is brought in and accused of being a civilian sneaking into the post. When he blames Bilko for ordering him to go AWOL, the General is ready to switch the object of the court-martial, but Bilko conceives an inspired defense: Zippo is the sole support of Chapman's family and therefore entitled to be released from the army as a hardship case. As relief spreads among the officers, Colonel Hall offers Bilko a rare warm moment: "I don't see how you did it." And they shake hands. The General then concludes the episode: "And remember: from this day on, you heard nothing" (here Captain Barker covers his ears), "you saw nothing" (now Colonel Hall covers his eyes), "you say nothing" (Bilko, looking at the camera, mischievously put his index finger to his lips and raises his eyebrows).

Like so many "Bilko" shows, this one hurtles breathlessly, a consequence primarily of Silvers' relentless force. Yet also present here is the quality that makes Bilko's intrigues loveable: a proverbial heart of gold. In another episode, for instance, a popular singer named "Elvin Pelvin" (modeled on guess who?) joins the platoon, and Bilko envisions making a fortune off him. But when the new man is overheard singing an endearing tribute to his sergeant, the eternal swindler can't bring himself to trade on the young man's talent.

Throughout the series he also demonstrated loyalty to his men. True, on every payday he seemed to concoct a new scheme, and at the first hint of it they tried to escape, only to be stopped in their tracks with an order such as "Freeze, you commandoes!" But Bilko ensured that no one else abused his litter, and not just financially. In "The Motor Pool Mardi Gras," for example, representatives from his platoon invite a local socialite named Joy Landers to serve as their queen. When she cruelly rejects them, Bilko takes her mockery as a personal affront: "Nobody laughs at my platoon." He then conducts an elaborate ruse to the effect that Doberman is an international playboy until, as Bilko predicts, Miss Landers begs to meet him. Doberman's greeting upon seeing his dream girl? "Drop dead." When newspapers report her humiliation, Bilko feels a twinge of remorse, but all resolves happily when Miss Landers visits the base, apologizes, and accepts their tribute.

Even Bilko and the Colonel had what might be termed "heart-warming" moments. In "The Transfer," Bilko is obliged to move to another camp, and initially Hall enjoys the repose. But when Bilko's replacement drowns the fort in regulations and paperwork, the Colonel yearns for Bilko's return. Meanwhile Bilko has found the pickings at his new base so easy that he wangles his way back to Fort Baxter. At first the Colonel smugly accuses Bilko of crawling, but when Bilko's girlfriend, Sergeant Joan Hogan (Elizabeth Fraser), reveals that the Colonel actually sought Bilko's return, the two men resume their battle, especially concerning authority over the Colonel's jeep. Suddenly, however, they smile, and Bilko says with genuine affection, "Nice to be back, sir." To which the Colonel responds with equal sincerity, "Nice to have you back, Ernie." Immediately the struggle of wills resumes, but the moment lasts in our memory.

The Phil Silvers Show and *McHale's Navy*

However warm Bilko occasionally became, what we all enjoyed most was watching him outwit the entire post. As when he threatened to write memoirs that supposedly would destroy countless careers. Or when he convinced the sporting world that the mighty Notre Dame football team would be defeated by tiny Schmill College. Or when he created a national inter-service wagering network over how many times a visiting woman lecturer would "twitch." The scams never ended, nor did Silvers' vigor.

When "You'll Never Get Rich" premiered, it ran against Milton Berle's variety show, heretofore the unstoppable NBC juggernaut. Within several weeks, though, the numbers reversed, and CBS had its own powerhouse. The show lasted four years and was still on top when the network, without Silvers' knowledge, canceled him. Apparently sustaining a budget with so many regular actors became impossible, and the network wanted to cash in on syndication.

"Bilko" proved to be the high point of Silvers' career. His next television venture, *The New Phil Silvers Show*, in which he played the aptly named Harry Grafton, lasted only a season. Later he rejected the lead in the original Broadway production of *A Funny Thing Happened on the Way to the Forum*, but after Zero Mostel triumphed in the role of Pseudolus, Silvers accepted a supporting part in the film version. He also took a major role in the Stanley Kramer comic extravaganza *It's a Mad, Mad, Mad, Mad World*, and among a cast that featured virtually every comedian in Hollywood, Silvers scored another triumph. In 1972, when *Forum* was revived on Broadway, he finally starred, but during the run suffered a stroke, and his health was never the same.

Ironically, for a man who achieved fame playing a card shark supreme, Silvers was a gambling addict, and lost hundreds of thousands of dollars in various activities. He was not always to blame, however. In 1967 a mob-inspired cheating scandal exploded at the gin rummy tables of the Beverly Hills Friars Club, and among the celebrated victims were Silvers, Zeppo Marx, Tony Martin, and shoe magnate Harry Karl, husband of Debbie Reynolds. In court, when asked how much he lost, Silvers commented, "Let's just say I'll be hitchhiking home."

Silvers died in 1985 at the age of seventy-four, but in Bilko he surely created a character that lives on.

Nat Hiken went on to create another fabled series, *Car 54, Where are You*, which starred two actors from "Bilko": Joe E. Ross, who played Bilko's perpetual dupe, mess Sergeant Ritzik, and Fred Gwynne, who had two memorable guest shots: as an expert on birds and as Ed "The Stomach" Honnigan, recruited by Bilko to win an eating contest. Hiken also brought with him some of the "Bilko" production team. The series ran for a couple of seasons, then faded. Hiken died of a heart attack at the age of fifty-four.

The legacy of service comedy, however, lived on, notably in *McHale's Navy*. One odd facet of this show was that Ernest Borgnine first played Quinton McHale in a straight dramatic piece, "Seven Against the Sea," about a PT boat commander and his stranded men who seek haven on a Pacific island and essentially go native. A more traditional officer, played by Ron Foster, parachutes down and tries to transform McHale's crew into a fighting force, but McHale, having seen so many men lost in battle, wants only to survive. In the end, though, he surprises everyone with his bravery. Originally shown on the ABC anthology series *Alcoa Presents*, the show received respectable ratings and was considered a likely candidate for a pilot, with the focus on Foster's upright character.

Instead, the project fell into the hands of Edward J. Montagne, fairly fresh from "Bilko," and he saw an opportunity to create another comedy about a freewheeling officer and his loyal unit. Borgnine confessed that initially he was reluctant to join the project, but after meeting a boy who was familiar with many television regulars, yet unable to recognize the Oscar-winning star, Borgnine enlisted.

During World War II he had served in the Navy, and after leaving the service without plans, followed his mother's suggestion to try acting. He achieved some stage success, but considerably more acclaim as a movie villain, notably in *From Here to Eternity* as the sadistic Sergeant "Fatso" Judson, who fatally beats the prisoner Angelo Maggio (played by Frank Sinatra, who won the Academy Award that resuscitated his own career). In *Bad Day at Black Rock* (1955) Borgnine torments the one-armed stranger (Spencer Tracy) who at the end of World War II visits a small Western town. Eventually Borgnine's character receives comeuppance in a thrilling bar fight with the soft-spoken war hero.

McHale's Navy took place in and around the island of Taratupa, just where the earlier drama was set. Here McHale and his men enjoyed interactions with natives who were either violent or shrewd, as well as with members of the Japanese military who commanded submarines, battleships, and fighter planes.

As noted earlier, Montagne brought not only actors from "Bilko," but also writers who understood the style and spirit he sought. Yet new ones

The Phil Silvers Show and McHale's Navy

made their mark, including one who contributed an early script under the name "Joe Heller." He was indeed the man who would one day create *Catch-22*, but for *McHale's Navy* he wrote a single episode that involves McHale's crew losing their boat, then stealing another one and repainting the number. Naturally the original vessel finds its way back, and confusion reigns. I don't think I'm out of place to suggest that such madness anticipated some of the spirit of Heller's fictional masterpiece.

Although Borgnine was officially the star of the show, two supporting players quickly stole center stage, as was indicated by a change in the title sequence. During the first season, the only actor pictured was Borgnine. By the second season, Tim Conway and Joe Flynn were shown together, and by the fourth and last season, each was featured individually.

When Conway joined the cast, he was a comparative novice. He had worked sporadically in Cleveland radio and television, until he was discovered by Rose Marie, then starring on *The Dick Van Dyke Show*. She brought him to the attention of Steve Allen, who for two years featured him among the company of comics (including Tom Poston, Don Knotts, and Louis Nye) on Allen's own weekly program.

Then came *McHale's Navy*. In the first episode, newly arrived Ensign Charles Parker, whose service record is already scarred with disasters, is ordered by Captain Binghamton to discipline McHale's roughhouse crew. They naturally resist, but McHale admires the bumbling but doggedly by-the-book young man, and convinces his men to play along. By the way, in that first episode McHale introduces himself to Parker by saying "Just call me Mac," but for the rest of the series no one did. As I've indicated, his crew called him "Skipper," while to the rest of the world he was "Quint" or "McHale."

As for Tim Conway's Mr. Parker, he was naïve yet gifted. He was childlike in his enthusiasm for adventure ("Gee, I love that kind of talk" he often said about Navy lingo), but he was also helpless with anything mechanical. Yet incompetence was not the only source of the laughter he provoked. When matters went awry, as they did in every episode, he waved his arms helplessly in the manner of Stan Laurel, or flinched with his entire body á la W. C. Fields. Yet Ensign Parker was also a skilled mimic who summoned a variety of dialects (English and French proved most useful), and thereby assumed a host of characters. He plunged wholeheartedly into each disguise, but could never resist correcting missteps and thereby compromising the illusion. Thus his masks were never convincing, but hilariously obvious.

And no matter how desperate a crisis might be, he could be distracted by trivia: ("You forgot to salute"). Thus he managed to make any silly situation sillier.

Nonetheless, his impersonations always fooled their main target: Captain Wallace Burton Binghamton, disparaged as "Old Leadbottom" by his men and portrayed unforgettably by Joe Flynn. At the start of the series, Flynn was gray at the temples and performed with an ill-tempered deadpan. Over the first season, though, his hair darkened, his gestures became more extravagant, and the register of his voice expanded. He also grew more conceited and desirous for promotion. Yet behind his framed glasses he remained a coward who met all annoyances with exasperation. When flustered, he resorted to bullying: "What are you talking about? Wha? WHA? WHA?" And at the end of almost every show, when he found himself defeated, he moaned to no one in particular, "Why is it always me?" (Shades of Duane Doberman). How to characterize the Captain's manner? To my mind he resembled a hyper-kinetic Jack Benny. Indeed, Flynn regularly manifested exasperation by resorting to one of Benny's most famous lines: "Now cut that out!"

No one episode of *McHale's Navy* stands out as the best, but I do have a favorite, for it sets Binghamton and Parker apart from everyone else and forces them to rely on each other. "Dear Diary" was written by two frequent contributors, William Raynor and Miles Wilder, directed by another, Sidney Lanfield, and originally aired on February 18, 1964.

The show opens in the crew's hut, where the men are making homemade hooch. Although all are equal in rank, their leader is Lester Gruber, played by the inimitable Carl Ballantine. Aside from acting on this show, Ballantine enjoyed a long career in vaudeville and nightclubs as a comic illusionist (or "magishun," as his onstage banner read). His rapid-fire patter reflected his shiftiness, and on this series he originated many of the crew's shenanigans. Yet occasionally he interrupted his sarong sales, liquor distributions, and poker sessions to perform feats of legerdemain. In this particular episode, the boys are concocting "Cloud Nine Martini Mix" in a hollow torpedo, but when McHale and Parker enter and realize what's happening, the Skipper lays down the law to his "schlockmeisters" (his favorite sobriquet for them). Yet even as he characteristically throws his arms straight up like Oliver Hardy, the mutual affection with the crew is obvious. Meanwhile Parker notes this latest escapade in his journal.

The Phil Silvers Show and McHale's Navy

When the men of the 73 embark on a mission, Binghamton and his aide, Lt. Carpenter (played by Bob Hastings) secretly motor up to the island. As they survey the crew's quarters for evidence, they come upon the torpedo and Parker's diary, and Binghamton recognizes that the boys are making martinis. Carpenter pointlessly asks whether they should search for olives, but the Captain figures that with the diary in hand, he has the requisite evidence to do away with McHale and the rest forever. Therefore he confiscates the book and prepares to take it to the Admiral.

Luckily for McHale, the Captain's plan is overheard by Fiji, a Japanese PW who secretly lives with and cooks for the crew of the 73. Here I should interject a side note. When the series began, enemy combatants were referred to as "Japs," but this label offended a significant number of viewers. Thus "Japs" was changed to "Nips," short for "Nipponese," and no more objections were heard. In this episode, when the crew returns, Fuji relates the Captain's scheme. And when Parker shamefully admits that he has recorded all of the crew's schemes, McHale realizes that they must retrieve the incriminating notebook, now locked in the Captain's safe.

Naturally Gruber volunteers to open it. He even refers to himself as "the little ol' safecracker, me," but this line is an anachronism because the phrase originated in a 1960s television commercial about "the little ol' winemaker, me." In any case, one problem remains because Carpenter will be guarding the safe. McHale, of course, has a solution: an order from the highest authority.

The scene switches to Binghamton's office, where an armed Carpenter zealously marches back and forth. When the phone rings, we move to Parker imitating President Roosevelt's patrician yet nasal inflection: "*My friend . . .*" and he orders Carpenter to summon the Captain. When the Lieutenant hesitates to leave his post, Parker asserts himself: "Get Captain Binghamton, or you won't be *my friend.*" The boys even imitate the President's dog, Fala, although the initial bark is too low for such a small pet. But a second, higher-pitched woof fools Carpenter, who dashes away, allowing Gruber to perform his burglary. When Binghamton returns, he giddily picks up the phone, full of deference to his commander-in-chief, but the line is dead. Binghamton can only fume: "I knew it wouldn't be him calling me. I didn't even vote for the man!" When the Captain sees the safe wide open, though, he overcomes his dismay and vows to trap McHale anyway.

Back at the island, McHale and the crew have burned Parker's diary. When the Captain bursts in and demands its return, McHale disclaims all knowledge, but Binghamton is undeterred: "I have a foolproof scheme. And here's the fool." He will make Parker testify, but the Ensign feigns a poor memory: "What is your name again?" The Captain tries to oblige: "Binghamton, Wallace—" then realizes that he is allowing himself to be distracted. He handcuffs himself to Parker, but unfortunately a window frame stands between them, and to free themselves the two men indulge in delicious physical comedy, with the Captain ultimately hopping out of the hut, still attached to Parker.

The next morning in Binghamton's office, after a sleepless night, spilled coffee, and additional slapstick, McHale offers to accept blame for all the illegalities described in Parker's diary, but Binghamton will have none of it, and he and Parker end up on a plane to COM.FLEET. Unfortunately an engine catches fire, so Parker puts on a parachute and prepares to jump. The flames extinguish themselves, but Parker follows the Captain's orders to sit and thereby falls out the open door, with the Binghamton left holding his leg. "I want my mother!" screams Parker, as they float down. "I'd like to get my hands on her myself!" wails the Captain.

They land on a Japanese held island, where Parker tries to free them from the folds of the chute: "Is that you, Captain?" To which Binghamton snaps: "Who do you think it is, Madame Butterfly?" Parker offers to bury the massive cloth, but Binghamton has an alternate suggestion: "Why don't you wrap yourself in it first?"

With the key to the handcuffs lost, the two fumble their way to a supply tent in search of a hacksaw. As the Captain searches, Parker inquires whether he's found anything. The reply is succinct: "Yes, I found a nitwit at the end of my left arm." Inside the tent they knock over some cans, then hide in a crate so as not to be discovered, but their hideaway is transferred to a plane bound for Tokyo. When the two force their way out of the large box, Binghamton invokes another reference to Oliver Hardy, that great man's eternal statement of mournful resignation to Laurel: "Here's another fine mess you've gotten me into." The handcuffed men create sufficient noise to bring out the Japanese pilot, but they manage to push him out of the plane, which they are left to fly on their own.

After they stumble through the door of the cockpit, Binghamton desperately asks what they should do first. Always the stickler for procedure, Parker responds: "Well, since there's no stewardess, we better fasten out seatbelts." Binghamton is naturally furious, but seconds later Parker finds what he thinks may be a useful dial.

The Phil Silvers Show and *McHale's Navy*

"Want me to turn this on?"

"What is it?"

"I think it's a heater."

That reply sends the Captain into another paroxysm.

Eventually McHale's crew locates the plane, and as it flies drunkenly, McHale's man shoots out an engine, setting this plane, too, on fire. Binghamton prepares to jump, only this time he wears the parachute. Parker, however, isn't quite ready to evacuate, for he is convinced that his flying skills have improved: "I think I'm getting on with it now." Soon, however, they land on the deck of PT-73.

Even after this harrowing adventure, Binghamton is still determined to take Parker to the Admiral. But when McHale reports that the Admiral plans an inspection tour for the next three week, and that Binghamton will have to spend that time chained to Parker, the Captain has doubts. Parker, on the other, isn't certain he wants to terminate the arrangement: "I think it's kicks." At this news the Captain tearfully relents, the handcuffs are sawn off, and life on Taratupa goes on. Sheer silliness, I know, but oh so funny.

One other episode from this series deserves mention: "The Seven Faces of Ensign Parker," also written by Raynor and Wilder. The premise is that thanks to another of the crew's thefts, Mr. Parker is caught with the Captain's new dictating machine, and the only witness is the Captain himself. To undercut Binghamton's testimony, the crew undertakes a campaign to make the Captain imagine that everyone he sees is Parker, so the Ensign moves from one disguise to another. Perhaps the most amusing is that of a nurse, who takes the Captain's pulse and announces "Quarter to two." The story couldn't be more ridiculous, but thanks to Flynn and Conway, with McHale keeping the enterprise rolling, the episode becomes a showcase.

Watching Parker and Flynn work together was a joy, for they functioned like an old-fashioned comedy team, seemingly in sync at every moment. Indeed, off-camera as well they looked like a unit. One of the treasures on *YouTube* is a brief film taken at the funeral of Stan Laurel on February 26, 1965. The mourners include some great names in Hollywood, including several whose comedy pedigree goes back to silent movies. Walking among that crowd, however, are Joe Flynn and Tim Conway, looking young, but very much as if they belong in such distinguished company. The voiceover during that montage, by the way, is that of Dick Van Dyke reciting "A Prayer for Clowns" as part of his eulogy for his idol, Stan Laurel.

After three seasons in the South Pacific, the crew of PT-73 transferred to Italy, where instead of "nips" they fought "jerries." The new setting permitted the introduction of local characters, including McHale's twin cousin, but the change of venue did not cure low ratings and plot repetition, so the fourth season was the last. Along the way the series inspired two feature films; both were in the same spirit as the series (although one manages without McHale), and both performed reasonably well at the box office.

After the show ended, the three stars followed very different paths. Borgnine continued his movie and television career, including an Emmy nomination for his performance at age ninety-two in the final episode of *ER*. He died in 2012 at ninety-five. Conway has continued working in television and movies, achieving perhaps his greatest success initially as a frequent guest on *The Carol Burnett Show,* then as a regular. That company included some enormously gifted performers, not to mention Burnett herself, but for me Conway's performances remain the high points. Burnett has related that the company used to shoot each script twice: first as written, then again to allow Conway to create additional foolishness. His two-man skits with Harvey Korman were especially brilliant. As Conway spoke in unexpected accents or inserted bizarre lines and actions, Korman struggled to maintain control, but more often than not collapsed with laughter. Because he never did so under other circumstances, and because the rest of the performers seemed equally vulnerable to Conway's madness, we may assume that such giggling was legitimate and contagious. Conway remains active today, guest starring on such shows as *Hot in Cleveland*.

After *McHale's Navy* Joe Flynn worked in television and in film voiceover, and even tried a new television project with Conway, but it faded quickly. Sadly, on July 19, 1974, he was found dead in his swimming pool, the apparent victim of a heart attack. Curiously, his death followed closely those of two other supporting stars of television: Frank Sutton, who played Sergeant Carter on *Gomer Pyle, USMC,* had died three weeks earlier, while Edward Platt, "Chief" on *Get Smart,* had died in March.

One last reflection. Decades after these two series ended, they were remade into movies: in 1996 *Sergeant Bilko* starred Steve Martin, and in 1997 *McHale's Navy* starred Tom Arnold. Neither film warrants further comment, except to note that they confirm how superb the original shows were.

Indeed, they remain a zenith of television farce. Although "Bilko" occasionally offered a glimpse of the bond between "Sarge" and his men, both series eschewed sentimentality. But thanks to gifted writers and even more gifted performers, these programs offered timeless and unadulterated nonsense for which I have never lost my affection.

III

Maverick
"Shady Deal at Sunny Acres"

and

The Fugitive
"Nightmare at Norfolk"

My early television heroes came in a variety of personae, but two of the most intriguing were created by one man: Roy Huggins, who also produced both of the series that featured these characters. He came to television comparatively late in life. Born in 1914, he graduated from UCLA in 1941 and during World War II worked in the U.S. Civil Service. After writing several novels, one of which he adapted for a script of the movie *I Love Trouble,* he toiled as a staff writer at RKO and Columbia, then moved into television at Warner Brothers as a producer. His efforts there and subsequently at Universal made him one of the bulwarks in the history of the medium.

Two of his best products, *Maverick* and *The Fugitive*, both featured men who traveled the country alone but found themselves involved with a succession of people and places. The natures of these encounters, however, were profoundly different. While the paths of the two Maverick brothers occasionally intersected, Bret and Bart lived independent from conventional society. They were drawn into social imbroglios only reluctantly, and if the effects of these stories were life-changing for some involved, the tone was usually light. In *The Fugitive*, on the other hand, Richard Kimble was a doctor and at one time very much part of what might be called "the establishment," but circumstance ripped his life apart and left him bereft of social moorings. Thus his nomadic existence demanded that he become immersed in the lives of others, and the implications of the narratives in which he starred were always dark.

Let's first consider *Maverick*, which was broadcast from 1957–62.

Before it came on the air, a lot of my time in front of the television screen was filled with old Westerns, grade C or D movies produced in the 1930s and 40s. They often aired in the afternoons on local New York channels, so after arriving home from elementary school at 3:00 or so, then spending my requisite time practicing the violin, I was free to indulge my enthusiasm for these adventures (homework was not yet part of the equation).

The films were technically primitive, and the only details I recall are the names of certain stars: Johnny Mack Brown, Bob Steele, Ken Maynard, and Hoot Gibson, all of whom faced similar challenges such as unscrupulous bankers or ruthless road agents. What set the good guys apart from the bad, aside from hat color, was an unerring sense of right and wrong, and I rooted accordingly.

To be fair, though, I didn't watch these films very closely. Rather I was more interested in acting out my own stories while the others played in front of me. The only television available rested before a large sofa, which I turned into an imaginary badlands. With my fantasy guns in hand, I would poke my head over an arm, then surreptitiously crawl over it, all in an effort to get the drop on unsuspecting villains, who were enacted passively by cushions. Sometimes I pretended that these decorative pieces had challenged me to a showdown. I don't want to boast, but rest assured that I was good. Not even once was I outdrawn by a pillow. And in those rare instances when we were forced into fisticuffs, I was equally effective. I used to take on two, sometimes three, pillows at once. Yet I always emerged victorious, and along the way saved plenty of besieged towns.

I also watched several contemporary Western series, and became a casual fan of a few. Roy Rogers and Gene Autry, for instance, had some appeal, but certain aspects of their shows displeased me. One, I didn't enjoy watching serious adventures interrupted by singing. Not that I didn't like singing, because I listened to music all the time. I just preferred my Westerns without musical interludes. Two, these shows sometimes featured modern contraptions like jeeps, which to my mind did not blend with horses. And three, these two heroes were burdened with comic sidekicks: Autry with Smiley Burnette and Gabby Hayes, Rogers with Pat Buttram. I understood the appeal of these fellows, who were likeable on their own, but, again, I found their buffoonery a distraction from the main thrust of the story.

Two Western series, though, worked for me. One was *The Cisco Kid*, starring Duncan Renaldo as Cisco and Leo Carillo as his best *amigo*, Pancho. I particularly liked the name of Cisco's steed, "Diabolo," as well as the show's thundering theme music. True, Pancho was a sidekick who provided levity, but he and Cisco both demonstrated mastery of weapons and horses, and therefore both earned my respect. Moreover, in my memory Cisco frequently outthought his enemies, and thus he was a tactician as well as a combatant. Finally, every episode seemed to end with these partners exchanging the same two lines: "Oh, Cisco," followed by "Oh, Pancho." Or maybe vice versa. Either way, they would then gallop off together, in rhythm with that terrific music. This weekly dénouement often inspired my brother and me to acknowledge each other in similar style: "Oh, Steven," I'd hail, to which he would respond, "Oh, Victor."

Nothing hysterical, I know, but we enjoyed ourselves.

The other series that I followed was *The Lone Ranger*, which presented another two men with skills aplenty. I particularly enjoyed the mysterious quality of the Ranger (played most of the time by Clayton Moore). To this day, his real identity remains the subject of controversy, but back then I learned that he was the "lone" survivor of a vicious attack by the Cavendish gang, that his last name was almost certainly "Reid," and that his first name was possibly "John." This inside knowledge made me feel omniscient. Furthermore, for reasons I don't care to contemplate, I also favored the Lone Ranger's mask, and acquired a cheap imitation that I wore from time to time during an enactment. Occasionally the Ranger removed his own mask, but at those times he turned away from the camera or hid his features under another disguise, often that of an aged prospector. Finally, I liked how at the end of each episode he disappeared without waiting for tributes from local beneficiaries of his efforts. For the Lone Ranger and Tonto, a job done well was its own reward, and such humility seemed to me befitting a hero. They didn't need grandiose declamations about how wonderfully they had performed.

I admired Tonto as well. He struck me as intelligent and resourceful, but also valuable on the trail, where he tracked other riders. My only confusion about him anticipated my career twenty years hence. I understood that English was his second language, and he communicated with it well, but he never grasped the essence of first-person singular. Why did he always say "Me go to the sheriff," when the Ranger and everyone around him said "*I'll* go to the sheriff"? Perhaps the producers of the series wanted to remind us that in their eyes Tonto could not function at the Long Ranger's level of sophistication. Whatever the reason, I resented how he was belittled.

The Lone Ranger also provided me with some of my favorite trivia. In addition to my awareness about the title character's real identity, I learned other esoteric bits that set me apart. Everyone, of course, knew the name of the Ranger's horse: "Silver." Fewer people knew the name of Tonto's horse: "Scout." Only a small group knew the name of the Ranger's nephew, who sometimes joined in capturing desperadoes: "Dan Reid." And virtually no one knew the name of Dan Reid's horse, but it was one I could never forget: "Victor," an offspring of "Silver."

Of course, for someone like me who relished good music, *The Lone Ranger* offered the best theme of all time. Even these days, long after the show has been off the air, can anyone hear the overture to the opera *William Tell* by Rossini and not think "Hi-yo, Silver"?

(*Hold on there, partner. The television show with the best theme music ever was Captain Video, which was introduced each week with the overture to Wagner's opera* The Flying Dutchman. *'Nuff said*)

My apologies for the interruption. We now return to the business at hand.

As I grew older, a couple of other Westerns caught my attention. One was *Gunsmoke*. I knew that the part of Matt Dillon had been offered to John Wayne, who had rejected it and suggested that his buddy James Arness be cast instead. I understood, too, that the show was skillfully done, and that the scripts aspired to a maturity rare in Western drama. Yet I could never become involved. The farmers and ranchers who inhabited Dodge City were truly dirty. Moreover, the characters and their issues were too complex for me to handle. What I failed to appreciate, of course, was that these characters and stories were comparatively realistic. In any case, throughout its legendary twenty-year run, I resisted *Gunsmoke*.

Have Gun—Will Travel offered different attractions. One was the main character of Paladin, a gunman for hire played by Richard Boone. Paladin was a West Point graduate who lived in San Francisco, spoke elegantly, and appreciated good food and appropriate wines. I didn't drink wine, but admired a cowboy who could handle himself in social circles. Furthermore, when Paladin hit the trail, he could respond as brutally as any cowpoke who dared challenge him. He also dressed in black like Zorro, and behaved according to a rigorous moral code. He hated gunplay, and when drawn into such conflict usually sighed heavily, as if to suggest that he regretted having to dispose of an opponent who was too much of a fool to realize that he didn't have a chance. Finally, Paladin had a card identifying himself: "Have Gun—Will Travel. Wire Paladin." Only after watching several episodes did I grasp that "wire" was not the hero's first name, but the means a potential client should use to contact him. Sometimes the subtleties of Paladin's moral judgments were beyond me, but I liked Boone's world-weary manner and his willingness to embrace the underdog.

I gave casual attention to other popular Westerns, such as *Cheyenne, Sugarfoot, Wyatt Earp, Lawman, Bat Masterson,* and *The Rifleman*. I wasn't a regular viewer of them, but when no other entertainment was available, these sufficed. Each presented a brave man who either moved from town to town (all of which looked remarkably alike), or stayed put to homestead and preserve the law. Either way, he dedicated himself to aiding troubled citizens, shooting dangerous ones, and romancing beautiful women who looked as if they had stepped out of a twentieth-century fashion magazine. Sometimes the questions of right and wrong were murky, but generally within each half-hour good triumphed and evil lost. I expected no less.

Then along came *Maverick*.

It was produced, as the opening of each program proudly proclaimed, by Warner Brothers, the same studio that offered many of those other shows (hence the similarity of the towns). But from the start *Maverick* was unique in several ways.

Most important, the title character was not a sheriff or a marshal. Nor did he lead a cattle drive or own a ranch. Nor was he trying to raise a family. Instead he meandered into town after town from New Orleans to San Francisco with no ambition other than to earn money playing poker, and the focus of his existence was the next game. On other shows and in movies, the polished dude playing cards was either slimy or peripheral to the main story. Here poker *was* the main story, at least until one or both of the Maverick brothers became involved with a beautiful woman or some other distraction.

One other note. That two brothers shared the lead in this series gave my own brother and me a special reason to enjoy it. We also found an additional form of salutation that we borrowed from the Mavericks: "Brother Steve" and "Brother Vic." One year my brother even brought me a unique birthday present: a book called *Poker According to Maverick*. You can still buy it.

Another key quality about *Maverick* was articulated by Huggins himself, who provided background to the show in Ed Robertson's entertaining volume *Maverick: Legend of the West*: "*Maverick* was not a 'comedy Western.' *Maverick* was a western with humor." (Robertson 19) In other words, at the series' basis was realism leavened with wit. Here was where the performance of James Garner as Bret Maverick was crucial. As Huggins explained, he saw Garner in a small role elsewhere, and realized at once that the actor had just the qualities essential for the character Huggins had in mind (Robertson 7). Good-looking and athletic, just like all traditional Western heroes, Garner had an ingratiating smile. Yet he also regarded neither himself nor the world around him seriously.

All other cowboy heroes overflowed with earnestness. Maverick exuded irony.

He never sought a gunfight, but if the situation warranted, he did not hesitate to shoot, and he did so effectively. He used his fists as well, but he was content to avoid brawls. In the face of an enemy, Bret just as easily shrugged as stared him down.

Yet the most important attribute that made Bret Maverick fascinating was an extraordinarily expressive manner, the same quality that helped Garner become one of the first actors to excel in both movies and television over a career that has lasted more than fifty years. Most cowboy heroes, indeed, most leading men, communicated only a few emotions: pride, fury, determination, and perhaps affection. Garner expressed these, but also managed frustration, bewilderment, sheepishness, and futility.

He was born James Bumgarner in Norman, OK, the youngest of three brothers. His mother died when he was five, and his father's remarriage caused the boy no end of unhappiness. At the end of World War II, sixteen-year-old Garner joined the Merchant Marines, but left because of seasickness. He joined his father in Los Angeles, where he attended school and eventually modeled bathing suits. Disliking the work, he returned to Norman, where he attended high school and played sports, then served in Korea and received two Purple Hearts. After his discharge, an actor friend persuaded him to take a nonspeaking role in the Broadway production of *The Caine Mutiny Court Martial*, and Garner often commented about how watching the nightly performance of the production's star, Henry Fonda, provided an education in acting. This engagement led to television and film roles, and after the studio billed him as "Garner," he made the name change legal. His biggest break before *Maverick* was opposite Marlon Brando in *Sayonara* (1957).

To this point I have scarcely mentioned the other title figure of the Maverick series, Bret's brother Bart, played by Jack Kelly. He came from a theatrical family, and his actress sister, Nancy, earned an Oscar nomination for *The Bad Seed*. Perhaps Kelly's most famous credit before *Maverick* was as a space traveler in *Forbidden Planet*, the 1956 adaptation of Shakespeare's *The Tempest*.

Kelly joined *Maverick* early in the first season when the pressures of filming an hour episode each week with Garner in virtually every shot proved impractical. Throughout the series Kelly offered wonderful moments, including several in the episode at the center of this chapter, but he lacked Garner's range, especially in matters of humor. Thus most of the shows that feature Kelly were closer to traditional, even serious westerns, while those that concentrated on Garner tended to be lighter. Thus for me, and I suspect for most fans of the show, *Maverick* means Garner. This attitude is like that of a large percentage of James Bond fans. They regard Sean Connery as the embodiment of the character, and any other actors in the part as imposters: skilled perhaps, even admirable at times, but ultimately inadequate. Yet Kelly's contribution to several *Maverick* shows should not be dismissed, and in "Shady Deal at Sunny Acres" he gives a superb performance.

Now to the episode itself. Roy Huggins found the germ of the plot in a volume by Joseph "Yellow Kid" Weil, a notorious con artist who operated out of Chicago in the late nineteenth century (Robertson 131). Apparently Huggins both developed the story and wrote the teleplay, but because Warner Brothers would not pay him for the two services, Huggins gave story credit to Douglas Heyes (Robertson 132). The script was directed with elegance by Leslie Martinson, who considered this episode to be the best constructed *Maverick* show (Robertson 101). Initially broadcast on November 23, 1958, it featured all the semi-regular or recurring characters who visited the series.

WALKING DISTANCE

The episode begins innocuously, as Bret Maverick strolls onto the screen from a familiar setting: the inside of a saloon. The manner in which he pats his wallet suggests that the evening has been profitable, and, indeed, he walks directly to the bank, where one light still burns. Seeing a man hunched over his desk, Bret taps lightly on the window. The man coldly informs him that the bank is closed, but Bret indicates that he wants to put money in, not take it out. At this news, the man cautiously opens the door while wielding a gun. Bret explains that he has $15,000 to deposit, and when asked how he acquired such a sum so late at night, replies in characteristic Maverick spirit: "Faith. In the friendly laws of probability." A second later he explains: "Poker." The banker cautiously counts Bret's money, then obliges the request for a receipt, and the transaction concludes harmoniously.

The next morning Bret tries to retrieve some of his money, but the banker, Mr. Bates (John Dehner), denies having seen him before. Bates's colleague, Ben Granville (Regis Toomey), confirms that the deposit form Maverick displays is obsolete; moreover, the signature does not match Bates's own. Maverick realizes he has been taken, but does not panic. Instead he explains the situation to Bates: "You owe me $15,000, and before I leave Sunny Acres, you're going to give it to me."

What is remarkable about these two scenes is the absence of violence or even the threat of it. In a normal western, guns would have been drawn by both sides, and a shootout would likely have occurred. Here we have nothing of the sort. We also note that Bret says that Bates "owes" him the money, not that Bates "stole" it.

The scene that follows, however, is even more special. We might expect Bret to work his way around town, menacing Bates or inveigling himself into the confidence of the townspeople. Instead, over some jaunty music, he settles into a rocking chair on the porch of the Sunny Acres hotel and begins whittling. As various citizens inquire about whether he has retrieved his money, Bret responds with a standard refrain: "I'm workin' on it." He then accepts the resulting mockery with a good-natured grin. During this sequence he is visited first by Bates and the Sheriff, but when Bates accuses Maverick of threatening him, Bret turns on his charm: "Why, I'm surprised at you, Bates." When the Sheriff warns Maverick that nothing bad had better befall Mr. Bates, Maverick amiably agrees. Garner plays this scene with an easy manner (he seems to lope sitting down), but just as the Sheriff is puzzled, so are we. What does Bret have in mind?

Maverick and *The Fugitive*

Our curiosity grows when Maverick is approached first by Ben Granville's daughter, who also suspects Bates of skullduggery, then that evening by Granville himself, who confirms that Bates has just paid $30,000 in cash to buy Granville's share of the bank. "Any way we can prove that some of that money is mine?" asks Bret. The answer is no, and Granville further warns that Bates is "tough, shrewd, and intelligent." Yet Granville, too, is puzzled. What is Bret's strategy? This exposition works wonderfully, as we join the citizens of the town in confusion.

We sense that something is up when the stagecoach arrives, and Bart Maverick steps out. Now, we assume, the two brothers will conspire. Yet Bart does not even acknowledge Bret, who continues whittling. And when Bart registers in the hotel, his signature reads "Bartley Mansfield II." The "II" is a superb touch, hinting at nobility or at least an upper-class affiliation. After the commercial break, we again expect to see the brothers in conference, but Bret hasn't budged: "I'm workin' on it" he tells a young reporter who inquires as to Bret's plans. A minute later Bart asks one of Bret's inquisitors about the location of "the old flour mill," and we are truly at a loss.

In the next scene, Bret is again visited by Bates, who by now has acquired a bit of a sneer: "Sunny Acres hasn't had such a laugh since Eddie Foy came to town two years ago." Bates also mentions that he carries a gun. Still, Bret's plan, if he has one, clearly does not involve violence. As Ben Granville noted, Maverick also does not intend to rob the bank. Fine, but what *does* he intend?

The answer begins to take shape when during Bart's evening meal, he is visited by Bates, who enters the dining room smoking a cigar and oozing confidence. He introduces himself to Bart: "I'd like to welcome you to our fair city." He also confesses that he has a second motive: he understands that "Mr. Mansfield" has expressed an interest in the flour mill, but adds that the bank has a lien on it. Bart is impressed by Bates's knowledge, but Bates remains humble: "It's a banker's business to know what's going on in his town."

Bart then lays out his situation. He claims to work for a group of British financiers who have hired him to purchase various sites. In response Bates claims that the price of the flour mill is $100,000, but Bart good-naturedly dismisses that offer. He will, however, consider $75,000. The deal is struck, and Bart reflects that he cannot remember completing a transaction so pleasantly.

Here, perhaps, is the place to acknowledge the casting in this episode. Whenever a *Maverick* script featured both Bret and Bart, Huggins would offer Garner the choice of which part that he, as Bret, wanted to play. For instance, here one brother propels the plot by suckering Bates, then traveling with him to involve all the other conspirators. Meanwhile, the other brother sits whittling and conversing. To Huggins' surprise, Garner selected the latter role, and the result is the episode that Garner himself has called his favorite because it's "Bret at his coolest" (Garner 63). The casting works for a couple of reasons. One, Bret always does his best work reacting to other people, particularly when he seems vulnerable. He also seems to approach every situation with a wink, and here the one who draws in Bates must do so with a straight, but smiling, face. Bart, on the other hand, is less colorful and less obviously a con man, qualities that diminish his effectiveness in other episodes, but which here work perfectly. He seems to be the embodiment of old world elegance; thus we understand why Bates would believe his patter.

One other performance deserves praise, and it is essential to the success of this episode: that of John Dehner as banker John Bates. Dehner enjoyed a long and varied career in radio, notably as Paladin in the radio version of *Have Gun—Will Travel*, and his career in movies and television lasted from 1945 until well into the 1980s. He often played smooth-talking scoundrels, appearing on countless series, among them *Gunsmoke* and *The Twilight Zone*, and from 1971–73 even played Doris Day's boss on *The Doris Day Show*. Here behind his cruel manner, he shows a faint touch of the ridiculous. Bart flatters Bates as "a man not to be easily fooled," but Dehner's performance, though Machiavellian, hints that Bates is so confident and manipulative that he is exactly the sort of man who *can* be fooled.

His portrayal also reminds us how in any story of crime, but especially revenge, a notable villain is vital. One example is *The Sting*, the 1973 caper film starring Paul Newman and Robert Redford, and which shares obvious qualities with "Shady Deal." The heavy in the movie, Doyle Lonnegan, played by Robert Shaw, is a cold-blooded killer with an ego to match his manner. He is therefore a legitimate target for the plot in which he becomes the victim. Bates does not present evil of such magnitude, but his sliminess invites retribution, and we're delighted to watch him fall into the trap that Bret and Bart set. In sum, a bona fide villain illuminates the bravery and cleverness of the heroes.

Soon we are back to the dining room, where Bates and Bart dine. Bates, ever vigilant, notices that Bart has been quiet, and wonders if their deal has fallen through. Bart assures him that all is well, but also that he is pondering a new opportunity, one worth millions. Bates is intrigued, but Bart insists that the matter must remain confidential. Pretending concern, Bates then offers his most memorable thought. Referring to himself humbly as Bart's banker, Bates advises, "After all, if you can't trust your banker, who can you trust?" The lesson here is that Bates is not invited by Bart to join the scheme. Instead Bates volunteers himself and is thereby permitted to think that he is the motivator. In other words, to catch a crook, create a situation wherein the crook may be inspired to utilize his crookedness.

As Bart draws closer to explain his "confidential" deal, Bates's face is a brilliant mask of false solicitude. Bart explains that the Nevada Empress Silver Mine, long considered barren, has been discovered to share lines with a far more lucrative vein. Therefore shares of the Nevada Empress, once useless, will soon amount to a fortune. Bart explains that he intends to buy ostensibly valueless shares for a pittance, then sell them for a massive profit. Bates is skeptical, but Bart assures him that the Denver banking firm of Schafer, Hill, and Ferris guarantees the plan. Moreover, Ralph Schafer happens to be a close friend of Bart, who by coincidence is leaving that afternoon for Denver to begin buying shares. We still cannot be sure where all this conniving is going, but when we hear that Bart's commission from the selling of the flour mill will be $7,500, we note that the sum is exactly half of what Bates owes Bret, who is out of sight for the moment, but still, we assume, whittling.

One other observation. Throughout the *Maverick* series, Bret and Bart quote their "ol' Pappy," a fount of cynical wisdom. Here Bart begins, "My old Pap—," then changes to "father" and adds "Sometimes a man must rise above principle."

The first stop in Denver is the home of a supposed widow named Carrie Watson, impersonated by an old rival of Bret's, Samantha Crawford (Diane Brewster). With her graceful Southern lilt, Samantha claims that honesty is the best policy, so she is reluctant to sell to these good-hearted men what she knows to be worthless stock. But Bart assures "Mrs. Watson" that as a speculator he takes such chances with the understanding that although many deals will fall through, some will turn a profit. As Bart offers five cents a share for 15,000 shares, "Mrs. Watson" looks astonished, because she never expected to earn that much. Here the camera catches Bates smiling with sickening sweetness. We also relish the bandying of words like "honesty" and "forthrightness" among these characters. When the transaction goes through, and Bart and Bates leave, Bart returns ostensibly for his hat, but in a wonderful comic touch, reminds "Samantha love" that she failed to replace in his pocket the entire sum that he has just paid to her. She admits her "teensie" mistake, and with a kiss they part.

Bates and Bart next visit the brokerage house of Schafer, Hill, and Ferris, where a clerk, impersonated by an old rival of Bart's, Gentleman Jack Darby (Richard Long), testily informs them that Mr. Schafer is in his private upstairs office. Bart and Bates dutifully walk up one flight, where they meet "Schafer" and his secretary, impersonated by two more old rivals, Dandy Jim Buckley (Efrem Zimbalist, Jr.) and Cindy Lou Brown (Arlene Howell). Initially Buckley feigns displeasure when he understands that Bates is privy to this confidential negotiation, but Bart explains that Bates is his banker, reassurance to which Bates adds his familiar maxim: "If you can't trust your banker, who can you trust?" Satisfied, Schaffer doles out a dollar a share, a full $15,000, while Bates practically salivates. Here again Dehner's face embodies a combination of stupefaction and greed.

When Bates and Bart leave, they do so with the announced intention of meeting a "Mr. Callahan," who supposedly has 100,000 shares of Nevada Empress. "Mr. Schafer" warns that "Callahan" will be a difficult character with whom to bargain. Here again, as throughout this script, we watch each member of the team lead their mark to the next contact. Thus we admire not only the ingeniousness of the scheme, but the smoothness of the performances (the one by the characters as well as that by the actors). We also appreciate the seamlessness of the story, so beautifully constructed that we accept that even a suspicious man like Bates would believe the ruse. After Bart and Bates leave, Buckley and Cindy exit their office and remove the nameplate on the door, revealing a "For Rent" sign underneath, then head off to meet Gentleman Jack. The scene parallels a similar gambit in *The Sting*, when members of the gang bring a painting order to an office where they have arranged a meeting with Lonnegan. After establishing contact, they instantly vacate, leaving the regular occupants at a loss.

Callahan, the owner of a hotel, is impersonated by another old cohort of Bret's, Big Mike McComb (Leo Gordon), who arranges to have himself paged while emerging from the real Callahan's office. "Callahan" initially dismisses both men, but when Bart persists, "Callahan" bitterly admits to owning 100,000 shares of Nevada Empress stock. When he inquires how

Maverick and *The Fugitive*

much Bart is willing to pay, Bates leaps in with "five cents a share," and we feel him tugging on the line, eager, even desperate, to share in the deal. "Callahan," however, scoffs at this offer, as well as at the ten cents a share Bart proposes. Finally "Callahan" states his terms: thirty cents a share for the entire 100,000 shares. Bart claims not to have the money, but "Callahan" gives him a week. Seized with determination, Bart leads Bates back to Sunny Acres.

Meanwhile we note the sum in question: $30,000, twice what Bates owes Bret.

Now the script offers an amusing interlude. Bates and Bart come upon Bret in his usual chair in front of the hotel. When Bates sarcastically asks if Bret has any more sayings, Bret acknowledges that in fact he does: "You can fool all of the people some of the time, and some of people all the time, and those are very good odds. My old pappy said that." As Bart ponders this remark and stares at Bret with curiosity, Bates assures him that Bret is "harmless," and Bates's self-satisfied sneer makes us anticipate his downfall more than ever.

Even the best of schemes, however, may meet a roadblock, and here comes the one for this episode. Bates checks his bank records, and discovers that one of his depositors, a Mr. Plunkett, owns 40,000 shares of Nevada Empress. Meanwhile Bart reports that his investors have turned down the $75,000 bid for the flour mill. Bates is willing to lower the price to $60,000, but Bart worries that his commission will be delayed, and that "Callahan" will drop his own offer. Bart expects Bates to suggest contributing his own money, but instead Bates proposes buying Plunkett's shares. To defuse the crisis, Bart delays visiting Plunkett, claiming to be bothered by a stiff collar. Bates is perturbed, but must wait.

The next scene takes us to Plunkett's farm, where Bates arrives with Bart. Bates cannot, he explains, give Plunkett the money for his shares now, but promises to return with it in a day or two. When Plunkett regretfully reports that the shares are with his daughter in "Californee," Bates is so intent to purchase them that he demands, "Where in Californee"? He then calms himself and pronounces "California" properly. Unfortunately, Plunkett explains, she has moved to Oregon. When Bart and Bates retreat, Bates offers to put up half of the money "Callahan" demanded for his shares: $15,000. He also insists that by allowing Bates to participate, Bart will earn a loyal friend. At last the entire plot comes to fruition. Still, Bart resists, asserting that he'll find another way, only to have Bates accuse him of being "hoggish." The irony is delicious. Not only is Bates willing to supply money of his own; he virtually blackmails Bart into accepting it. Bart agrees that he has "no choice," to which Bates affirms, "That's the spirit!"

When the two ride off in the buckboard, Bret emerges from the barn to pay Plunkett $100 for his complicity and to assure him that the Nevada Empress stock indeed has no value. Bret adds that Plunkett would never have seen the $4000 Bates promised, and Plunkett laughingly agrees. Everyone understands that Bates is a crook.

Back in Denver, Bates and Bart complete their transaction with "Callahan." To Bates' consternation, Bart accepts "Callahan's" invitation to dine, while Bates heads up to "Shafer's" office. Meanwhile Bart and Big Mike enjoy a laugh, the money is directed back to Dandy Jim, and Bart is off to find his horse and return to Sunny Acres before Bates can arrive.

Now the dénouement unfolds quickly.

With "Callahan's" shares in hand, Bates rushes upstairs to what he remembers as Shafer's hideaway, but instead finds the "For Rent" sign. He then hurries back to the main office, where he is told that Mr. Shafer has retired, not surprising for a man of eighty-one. Dehner's response to this news is priceless: not just the words ("$15,000. He did it."), but the sickly, mournful expression across his face.

Back in Sunny Acres, Bart prepares to leave. He passes Bret on the porch, still whittling, but the two do not acknowledge each other. Instead Ben Granville asks Bart if he's met Mr. Maverick, but Bart has time only to suggest that Mr. Granville check the bank's funds. The next shot is of the morning paper headline: "Mystery Embezzlement by Banker Bates," and the opening lines of the article indicate that Bates has stolen $15,000. As the townspeople rally to bid Bret goodbye, the reporter who earlier sought to know Bret's plans solicits a comment, but Bret responds simply: "My business in Sunny Acres is finished." The sheriff, however, demands a fuller explanation. With a smile Bret, already on the stagecoach, hands him the wood-carving that now looks like a donkey (a symbol of Bates?) and offers these words: "Sheriff, it's not often I can say this, but I feel like I'm leaving Sunny Acres a better place than I found it." And he's gone.

Against some delightful music, the townspeople look at one another, then at Bret's chair, then at the bank, and then back to one another. They have no idea what's happened.

Perfect.

Maverick and *The Fugitive*

Roy Huggins himself discussed how this episode anticipated the opening of *The Sting*. We should also note that Huggins used the same basic plot structure in two scripts from a later series of his, *The Rockford Files*, which also starred James Garner: "There's One in Every Port," written by Stephen J. Cannell, one of Huggins' protégés, and "Never Send a Boy King to Do a Man's Job," written by Juanita Bartlett. (The former show, by the way, features John Dehner, this time as one of Garner's allies.) But in these scripts we are denied the joy of discovery; instead the audience watches the plot being hatched. Inevitably twists occur, but basically from the start we know the goal and the overall strategy. The special charm of "Shady Deal" is that the audience remains mystified for quite a while, and only gradually do we learn the point of what unfolds.

Before closing this section on *Maverick*, I should mention two more favorite episodes of mine. One is "Gun Shy," broadcast later in that same season and which turned out to be one of the most watched television shows of the year. It's a giddy parody of *Gunsmoke*, but not entirely successful, for the satire is sometimes heavy-handed. Still, that such a take-off could exist and earn such viewership is evidence of the influence of *Maverick*. The other episode is "Greenbacks Unlimited," which ran in the third season. Bret is hired by local officials to catch a safecracker whose name and face are unknown. All they know of him is that has the reputation of playing cards, and as the marshal suggests, "It takes a thief to catch a thief . . ." At this faint praise, Bret is a mite offended, but accepts the job for a promised fee of $1000 if the thief is caught. While on the job, Bret runs into an old friend, Foursquare Farley, whose living quarters include a wall that opens inside the Denver Bank vault. Subsequently a poker player who attracts Maverick's attention turns out to be the wanted criminal, Big Ed Murphy, played by none other than John Dehner in another superb performance. Eventually the two stories intertwine, Murphy and his two confederates are caught, and the result is a program that *The Hollywood Reporter* called "the funniest show of the year."

At the end of *Maverick*'s third season, contract disputes between Garner and Warner Brothers led to Garner's leaving, and although the series continued for two more years with Kelly and later Roger Moore as Beau Maverick, the unique quality that Garner injected could not be recaptured. Still, the first three seasons are as enjoyable today as they were more than fifty years ago. Garner, as I mentioned earlier, continued with an extraordinary career in movies and television, the highlights of which are too numerous to be mentioned here.

Huggins, meanwhile, embarked on a new series, but one very different in tone.

The theme of a lone man wandering around the country is familiar in American fiction and film, but we would struggle to find two more contrasting treatments of the premise than in the two television programs considered here. Whereas *Maverick* injected wit and even fun into conventional Western plot elements, *The Fugitive* brought to crime drama an overpowering existential isolation. Dr. Richard Kimble was convicted of murdering his wife, but as the opening of each episode reminded us, he was innocent. On the way to execution, however, the train that carried him crashed, Kimble escaped, and thereafter he continued to run, impelled by two goals. The first was to catch the one-armed man he saw leave Kimble's house before he came home to find his wife dead; the second is to avoid capture and death. In the meantime he took whatever jobs he could find, perpetually fearful of revealing too much about himself. Therefore he avoided pictures, the police, and intimate contact with just about anyone. And whenever discovery loomed, as it did in every show, he took off down the road. Any road.

One real-life inspiration for the series was Sam Sheppard, an Ohio doctor accused of murdering his wife, but acquitted in a second trial. Still, the plot device of an innocent man seeking asylum is familiar, perhaps most notably in movies of Alfred Hitchcock such as *The Thirty-Nine Steps* and *North by Northwest*. Another possible forerunner of a fictional doctor who finds temporary haven in disguise was the movie *The Greatest Show on Earth*, in which James Stewart as Buttons the Clown remained in makeup throughout the film. Even more interesting, what propelled Buttons to reveal his medical skills and thus his identity was a life-threatening injury to the circus manager. Such was the sort of ethical dilemma Richard Kimble encountered regularly throughout *The Fugitive*.

Kimble was portrayed by David Janssen, who until this series was best known for playing the title role in *Richard Diamond, Private Detective*. He was born in Nebraska as David Meyer, but after his parents' divorce moved with his mother to Los Angeles, where as a child actor he took the name of his stepfather. Janssen's gruff voice and clenched manner were already evident in the first series, but *The Fugitive* allowed him to exercise a variety of idiosyncratic gestures and tics that became indelible to Kimble.

The character of Lt. Philip Gerard, the police officer determined to recapture Kimble, was based loosely on Javert, the police inspector from

Victor Hugo's novel *Les Miserables*. What made Gerard, played by Barry Morse, compelling was that Kimble escaped Gerard's own custody, and now the Lieutenant was, in the words of the weekly opening, "obsessed" with carrying out justice for not only the state but also for himself. In addition, on several occasions during the series Gerard faced the possibility of Kimble's innocence, but pushed that matter aside. Gerard's prime responsibility outweighed all other considerations.

Much has been written about themes and implications of *The Fugitive series*. One of the most extensive studies is by Stanley Fish, who in *The Fugitive in Flight: Faith Liberalism, and Law in a Classic TV Show* explores what he sees as the show's philosophical, ethical, and even theological implications. Fish makes a number of provocative points, some of which I'll consider in the discussion of "Nightmare at Northoak," but when I watched the series decades ago, I was involved more with characterization and dramatic technique, and these aspects have remained at the forefront of my reaction.

Some of my concerns are, I admit, trifling. How did Kimble manage to stay so well groomed? He was always closely shaved, with his hair combed and trimmed, as if he had stepped out of a barber shop. He often wore a jacket and tie, and had an endless supply of small, but occasionally spiffy, luggage. How could he afford those accoutrements? What supplies did he carry with him, and how did he manage to find places to sleep and eat? How did he perform his ablutions and other rudimentary tasks of survival?

I also thought about him on a more sophisticated level. Kimble often rode buses, which have always seemed to me to be the most lugubrious manner of transportation. Planes offer glamour, trains dignity, and cars independence, but a bus pulling out of a terminal with passengers huddled near one another has always struck me as sad. I'm sure other folks feel differently, but during my own bus trips, and I've actually enjoyed quite a few, I always think how many of my fellow passengers seem like relatives of Richard Kimble.

As indicated, Kimble was not only a trained pediatrician, but also had a number of other skills. He was a superb mechanic, especially with cars and trucks, but additionally he steered boats, cared for animals, and manipulated an endless variety of machinery and gadgets. As if all these gifts were not enough, he was handy with his fists.

Certain patterns of dialogue became familiar, for throughout the show's run (1963–1967), much of the language was saturated with repeated words and phrases. No matter the circumstances, one character after another spoke about "fate," "guilt," "fear," "loneliness," "crime," "identity," "justice," "love," or "escape." I'm no doubt omitting a few, but together they encapsulated the themes of Richard Kimble's life.

Finally the dramatic underpinnings of the show challenged viewers. We were aware that Kimble would not be caught, because that result would end the series. We also knew that he couldn't bring the one-armed man to justice, because that event, too, would terminate everything. Thus as suspenseful as each near capture might be, the series couldn't be played strictly for plot. It had to offer more, and it did.

The situation was rather like Shakespeare's *Romeo and Juliet*. In that play's Prologue, the Chorus announces what events will unfold: "A pair of star-crossed lovers take their life . . ." From that point on, our concern will be not the resolution of the story, but the reasons the story resolves as it does. The Chorus adds about the two leading characters: ". . . with their death bury their parents' strife." In other words, the most important point is that the suffering of these young lovers will change the lives of others.

The same principle applied to The *Fugitive*. We become absorbed not by the *what* of the story, but by the *why* and the *how*. Most episodes dramatized Kimble trapped in a seemingly hopeless predicament, and we were glad to see him escape, but the truly powerful shows, and we can find many, are those in which individuals who interacted with Kimble were transformed.

Such is the case with "Nightmare at Northoak," written by Stuart Jerome, directed by Christian Nyby, and originally broadcast on November 26, 1963. It begins with the opening that initiated every episode during the first season. As a train roars from darkness into light, we hear the booming voice of William Conrad explains the show's premise: Dr. Richard Kimble is on his way to execution, but is innocent. Conrad then intones: "But in that darkness, fate moves its huge hand." The line sounds close to the concluding words from the *film noir* classic *Detour*: "Whichever way you turn, fate sticks out a foot to trip you." The similarity reminds us of the close relationship between *The Fugitive* and the *film noir* tradition. Both dramatized the plight of a lonely drifter (almost always male), living in shadow, trapped between both memory and nightmare and a past and a future that were each dangerous. He lived on the edge of a society that was usually hostile, often corrupt, and rarely comforting. The only traditional element of *film noir* not endemic to *The Fugitive* was the duplicitous female who led the protagonist to his disastrous end. In the television series we met a few

Maverick and *The Fugitive*

such figures, but most women Kimble encountered manifested sympathy for him, even when they learned his true identity.

This episode begins in archetypal *noir* style, as the hunched figure of Richard Kimble walks alone down the dark street of an unnamed town. Behind him he hears the steps of a pursuer, so he ducks into an alley. The pursuer turns out to be Gerard, so Kimble dashes into yet another alley until he is trapped. Gerard, looking even more obsessed than usual, finds Kimble and pulls a gun with the words "Finally, Kimble," then shoots him.

The shot wakes up Kimble from what we realize has been a recurring nightmare. The actual sound is a tire blowout, and it comes when a busload of children careens wildly, the driver unconscious at the wheel. Eventually the bus stops and almost immediately bursts into flame. With no regard for his own welfare, Kimble pulls the door open and releases the children, fighting through flames twice to rescue wounded stragglers. An explosion from the bus, however, sends him flying. We remember that Kimble was a pediatrician, and during the series he often met children upon whom he bestowed kindness and medical help. Here the ones he rescues pull him to safety.

Kimble awakens in a bed. We might suspect he is in a hospital, but in fact he is in the private home of Al Springer, whom we and Kimble soon learn is the local Sheriff. At the moment, a beneficent doctor tends to Kimble. No identification was found on him, but everyone assumes it was burned in the fire. Meanwhile the townspeople gathered in the living room of this house are concerned about the hero who saved their children. One offers to pay his bills, another wants to bring him a bottle of wine, and yet another offers to bring him home-made jam, but the doctor advises that what the man needs most is rest. The overall vision is of a benign, almost fairy-tale, small town in New England, probably the way most Americans like to think of themselves. Everyone appears comforting, and warmth pervades the room. As we shall note presently, such is not always the vision in this series.

The one discordant note is sounded by Mrs. Springer, played by Nancy Wickwire. When someone comments that the accident appears to be no one's fault, Mrs. Springer contradicts her: "Accidents are always someone's fault." And she is determined to find the cause. "Right is right." Her certainty at this moment, and her determined manner when speaking to the other women of the town as well as with her husband, suggests that she will lead to a key theme of the entire series: ". . . the distinction between the letter of

61

the law (which has been established as a matter of legal fact) and the spirit of the law (what is really true despite the weight of evidence)" (Fish 37).

This conflict has a far-reaching dramatic heritage, including plays of Shakespeare. In *The Merchant of Venice*, for example, Shylock repeatedly craves the "letter" of the law, while Portia, among others, urges him to temper justice with mercy. In that play, to be sure, Portia and the Venetians prove brutal in their own right, and the dramatic matrix is complicated by anti-Semitism and the greed and vengeance that underlie the city. But the question of the nature of justice is familiar, and Mrs. Springer will face it most directly. Thus as Fish notes, this story belongs as much, or maybe more, to Mrs. Springer than it does to Kimble, whose role becomes comparatively passive. The Sheriff himself presents a sympathetic demeanor, no surprise because he is played by Frank Overton, who also portrayed Martin Sloan's compassionate father, Robert, in "Walking Distance," the episode from *The Twilight Zone* considered earlier.

The next potential threat to Kimble is a local photographer, who seeks to bribe the Springers' son to take a picture of the sleeping hero. The photographer's purpose, he claims, is "to do something for him. To make him famous." The irony of this line does not escape us, for Kimble is already more famous than he would prefer. We, however, note the ruthlessness of the photographer, who pretends to care about promoting Kimble as hero but seeks to promote himself first. He embodies many of the journalists in this series, for whom the scoop is paramount and the human being incidental. In this instance, as Kimble lies unconscious, a cloth partially covers his face, but the picture the boy takes ends up in the newspaper anyway.

When Kimble awakens, he speaks with the Sheriff and his wife, who still have no idea who he is. As Kimble identifies himself as "George Porter," and struggles to explain how he happened to be in Northoak, we see the familiar characteristics that make Kimble such an intriguing presence. Janssen is handsome, but even in roles other than Kimble, and even when he smiles full out, he always seems possessed by terminal melancholia. Here his crooked half-smile, almost a flinch, and his habit of looking away from anyone with whom he speaks are evident, and whenever he is onscreen he tends to withdraw into himself. All these mannerisms reflect fear of discovery, but though they might be obvious, they are effective. At the end of this brief conversation, Mrs. Springer brings "Porter" breakfast while the Sheriff departs for work, but not before Kimble sees the telltale badge pinned to his uniform. Kimble nonchalantly inquires as to Springer's occupation, and the revelation that Springer is Sheriff plants a seed in Kimble's mind. So does the sight of his half-covered face in the newspaper. Springer's own gentle ways are again counteracted by those of his wife, of whom he jokingly says: "I call the little woman the real Sheriff of Oak County." She affirms his judgment: "I stick by the letter of the law. My father was a judge." The crisis she shall soon encounter is thus established.

Desperate to avoid confrontation, a weakened Kimble struggles out the window and tries to run away. Meanwhile Gerard, having seen the picture of "Porter," guesses the identity of the subject and calls for fingerprints. While Gerard waits for a reply, Kimble, still dizzy from his concussion, falls unconscious, only to be found by boys who see an opportunity to repay their town hero. The irony that we have seen throughout this episode thus recurs, as acts of generosity, here performed by the youngest citizens, create trouble.

Back in the Springer household, Kimble cannot explain his attempt to escape, but neither the Sheriff nor Norma thinks much of it. That is, until the Sheriff reluctantly follows orders from Gerard and takes Kimble's fingerprints. At that moment, Norma picks up the newspaper and suddenly intuits why "Porter" ran away. With no option, Kimble confesses the truth, but claims innocence. Mrs. Springer's next question is at the heart of the episode: "Was it a fair trial?" The crucial word is "fair." If a wrong verdict was reached, can a trial ever be "fair"? Kimble admits in his typically hesitant manner, "Well, legally, yes." That's all she needs to hear. When he asks for help, she rejects him, but his next line stops her short: "Is that too much to ask? A life for a life?"

He saved her son. Doesn't she owe him? So we ask ourselves.

The anguish Mrs. Springer undergoes is apparent, especially when her husband disparages the demand for fingerprinting because "Porter" is "my kind of man," then adds "he knows I'm just doing my job." The line is an uncomfortable echo of Gerard's convictions in several episodes. At that juncture Norma cannot help but reveal the truth: "It's right, it's right," she mumbles, half to herself. Doe she mean the report, or the action she is about to take? "He is Richard Kimble," she struggles to say. The Sheriff then opens the bedroom door to find "Porter" attempting once again to escape through the window. Trapped, Kimble offers his hands for cuffing, but the Sheriff dismisses such humiliation. As the two men, leave, tears drip down Norma's face. Viewers, of course, sympathize with Kimble, but we also understand that Norma has followed her deepest values. Yet under what circumstances should good values be superseded by others?

When the Sheriff drives up to the station with Kimble in the front seat, a crowd observes them. We wonder how all these people appear at once, but the sense of community support for Kimble is convincing. As the Sheriff leads Kimble to jail, the camera ominously recreates the feeling of a "last mile." Lying on a cot, Kimble experiences the same nightmare that started this episode; only this time when he awakens, Gerard is standing there for real, with the same determined look we have come to know. One curious aspect of Barry Morse's performance, or perhaps the word is "appearance," is that even when his face is in repose, the ends of his mouth turn down, so that he looks more obsessive than he might normally. Back in the main office, Gerard hands Springer a letter of extradition that requires the Sheriff's signature. Kimble will then be escorted by another officer to the State Attorney General and thereafter released in Gerard's custody. Springer's resentment is evident in every gesture, while his deputy speaks with bile toward Gerard, but the two men grimly fulfill their responsibilities. We realize that Gerard is not the only one who "obeys the law."

With the officer not expected back for three hours, Springer invites an admittedly hungry Gerard home for dinner. There, while consuming his meal, Gerard recounts his past efforts to recapture Kimble, but his manner is gleeful, bordering on smug, and more than ever we want him to be thwarted. Suddenly the Springer son bursts into tears and confesses that he took that incriminating picture, and is therefore responsible for Kimble's imprisonment. His parents are shocked, but neither blames him. Gerard even suggests that Mrs. Springer should assure the boy that he did "the right thing. Just as you know that you did." Again the dialogue hinges on the meaning of the word "right." Mrs. Springer then asks if Kimble has any chance of receiving mercy, but Gerard, ever honest, shatters that hope.

As the scene continues, we observe Mrs. Springer turning away from her previous values: "Lieutenant . . . did he kill his wife?" Gerard answers brusquely: "The law says he did." Mrs. Springer persists: "What do you think?" Again Gerard ducks the question: "The law says he's guilty. I enforce the law." Mrs. Springer then reaffirms what has always been her core belief: "What's right is right." Gerard tries to bolster her spirit: "I suppose you could put it as simply as that." Here Mrs. Springer looks deep within her own conscience: "I have. All my life."

Gerard's return to the jail is one of the key scenes in the series. After the Sheriff and his deputy reluctantly obey Gerard's next directives, the Lieutenant looks in on Kimble. "How you must hate me," Gerard says. When Kimble declares his innocence, Gerard accuses him of lying; at this moment he does not bother hiding behind the cloak of duty. Then Kimble makes an accusation of his own, and speaks of the one-armed man that Gerard rejects as a phantom: "Your nightmare is that when I'm dead, you'll find him." Gerard has no reply, but the line clearly stings.

At this juncture the Sheriff requests that members of the town be allowed to bid farewell to the prisoner. Gerard is not pleased, but under his supervision (and the Sheriff's), familiar visitors file by to shake Kimble's hand. Some offer oral gratitude. The last visitor is Mrs. Springer, who sneaks a key into Kimble's palm. As she stands right under her husband's gaze, we wonder if he notices.

Minutes later, with the Sheriff gone home and the jail deserted except for one deputy, Gerard checks once more on his prisoner and sees only a figure under a blanket. As he opens the cell, he is knocked unconscious by a hidden Kimble, who takes Gerard's gun, locks the deputy in the cell, and run off into the night.

The Epilogue occurs the next day without him, but in front of all the men and women who visited the previous day. Facing down a crowd outside the jail, Gerard confronts the Sheriff, insisting that the Springer gave Kimble the key and threatening retribution from authorities. Mrs. Springer, however, insists that she is the guilty one. A shocked Gerard transfers the threat to her, but then, in what Stanley Fish calls a "Spartacus" moment (Fish 40), every member of the group claims to have helped Kimble free himself. In the face of such intransigence, a helpless Gerard leaves, while Springer gazes with admiration on his wife. Did he see her give Kimble the key? We don't know, but we do understand that she has been transformed.

The unification of the townspeople behind Kimble is one of the inspiring moments of the series. Indeed, the entire episode has a benevolent spirit. Other shows, however, portray a much darker side of rural America. One of the harshest is "Corner of Hell," broadcast near the end of the second season. Here, against the advice of local police, Gerard chases Kimble into a heavily wooded area inhabited by hostile moonshiners. These are not the good-natured mischief-makers of countless comedies, but paranoid malcontents suspicious of all strangers, especially those with badges. Kimble has aided one of their injured members, so when Gerard invades seeking the man they call "Doc," their antipathy is exacerbated. When Gerard is wrongly accused of attacking a local girl, he is sentenced to death, and after insisting that he saw an unidentified figure skulk away, begs Kimble to save him. The irony of his claim is both terrifying and touching. As Gerard pleads, his eyes open in acknowledgment of how his reality parallels that of Kimble; meanwhile Kimble's expression turns slightly mocking at recognition of how the two have switched places. Eventually Kimble uncovers the truth, and Gerard is freed, but his escape out of this pit of savagery becomes our own.

A more optimistic, yet equally resonant episode is "All the Scared Rabbits," broadcast in the third season. Suzanne Pleshette plays Peggy Franklin, a recently divorced woman who hires Kimble to drive across the country with her and her daughter, whom Peggy has abducted from her estranged husband. Unbeknownst to the adults, the little girl has taken from her father's laboratory a rabbit infected with meningitis, and soon she falls dangerously ill. To save her, Kimble must use his medical skills, thereby further arousing the suspicions of a marshal who has been following him. When the girl recovers, the marshal, moved by Kimble's courage and compassion, ignores police reports and releases him. Meanwhile Peggy resolves to win back her child by legal means. Thus Kimble profoundly alters the lives of at least three people. One irony of casting here: the marshal so stirred by Kimble's actions is played by R. G. Armstrong, who also appeared as the leader of the repulsive moonshiners in "Corner of Hell."

As *The Fugitive* drew to its close, Gerard's attitude toward Kimble softened. In one late episode, "Ten Thousand Pieces of Silver," Gerard and a squad of trooper have encircled Kimble and, unbeknownst to them, another man on the run. One of Gerard's posse shoots at what he assumes is Kimble, but Gerard stops him. The officer is confused: "You said he's a killer." But Gerard answers, "No, I said he has killed. There's a difference."

Finally, we must mention the closing two-part episode of the series, "Judgment Day." Some critics have complained that it falls short because Gerard himself does not unveil the entire truth about Kimble. Instead, circumstances bring Kimble and the one-armed man, Fred Johnson (played by Bill Raich), back to Kimble's home town of Stafford, Indiana. Kimble and Johnson finally meet atop a tower at an amusement park, where Kimble in fury beats Johnson until he confesses to the murder. Johnson threatens to kill Kimble, but Gerard shoots Johnson, who falls to the ground dead. As Kimble and Gerard stand over the body Gerard warns that Johnson's

Maverick and *The Fugitive*

confession will be useless in court, but finally Kimble's neighbor, Lloyd Chandler, appears. Gerard knows that Chandler witnessed the murder of Helen Kimble, but out of shame for his inaction has remained silent. Earlier Gerard placed the facts squarely before Chandler: "For four years we, both of us, kept an innocent man in hell." We feel the torment that Gerard himself feels. At last Chandler confesses the truth and swears to do so at the trial.

The Epilogue here is also the Epilogue to four years of shows, but it is appropriately austere. Kimble emerges from court a free man, only to face more questions from an insatiable press. When he and Gerard confront each other, they stare and shake hands but exchange no words. At that moment a police car drives up, and Kimble instinctively tenses, but Jean, the woman who has befriended him, says a simple "Hey." Kimble returns the greeting, offers a familiar half-smile, and walks off with her. The narrator concludes: "August 28th. The day the running stopped."

The final episode was a national catharsis. Even today, any viewer could easily imagine an entire country exhaling with relief, as 72% of American homes were tuned in, a record unsurpassed until the "Who Shot J.R." episode of *Dallas*, then by the closing episode of *M*A*S*H*.

I confess my own fantasy about the ending of the series. I like to imagine Kimble revisiting all the people whose lives he touched, and whom he left wondering how he would survive. I try to picture how those reunion scenes might play out, and I even imagine another series based on such visits. Then I tell myself that those figures will read his story, and thereby experience their own closure.

The Fugitive remains a remarkable creation. Each week the title character literally faced life and death. He formed occasional alliances, but none could be more than temporary. Try as he might, he could never escape himself and his personal limbo. Meanwhile many of the characters he encountered were almost as desperate as he, enduring crises that often reflected the intellectual isolation and emotional uncertainty that haunted America of the 1960s. Thus the rootless stranger found himself trapped amid social upheaval, and the results were usually intriguing and often memorable.

I would suggest one other reason why millions of viewers tuned in every week to see Richard Kimble's struggle: we identified with him. Few of us were on the run, of course. I certainly wasn't, but I could not help wondering how I might handle myself under such pressure. How would I survive? How would I function picking fruit twelve hours a day or working in a desert mine? I even contemplated how I would withstand a police interrogation or intense questioning by a suspicious employer. At the same time, Kimble's life embodied a degree of romance; after all, he wandered free from all the mundane aspects of existence that burdened the rest of us. For a timid soul like me, Richard Kimble was a fantasy alter ego. The experiences he underwent were frightening, but from the serenity of home I enjoyed sharing them.

By the third year of its run, *The Fugitive* dropped out of the twenty top-rated programs. The fourth season was shot in color, but concurrently, most fans believe, the quality of the scripts dropped. Equally important, David Janssen was understandably exhausted, for he was the focus of every show and required to be in virtually each scene. The last episode was, as indicated, a national event, but by then the series had exhausted everyone.

In 1993 a film version was released, starring Harrison Ford as Kimble and Tommy Lee Jones as Gerard (Samuel, not Philip). Jones won the Oscar for Best Supporting Actor, and this version of the story remains popular on television. Here Kimble does not scramble aimlessly across the country but rather hides in Chicago trying to solve his wife's murder. We know he'll succeed, but the story still works.

After *The Fugitive*, David Janssen went on to star in two more television series: *Harry O* and *O'Hara, U.S. Treasury*. He was also featured in several movies. Nonetheless, *The Fugitive* remains the summit of his career. On February 13, 1980, he suffered a fatal heart attack at his home in Malibu. He was just forty-eight.

Roy Huggins continued to produce, and another of his creations became a television classic: *The Rockford Files* (1974–1980). This series may be regarded as an amalgam *of Maverick* and *The Fugitive*, for it starred James Garner, who brought his same seemingly effortless excellence, but also featured a detective who battled forces of American corruption. Huggins died in 2002, but his legacy is unchallenged: shows that brought to television, and to American culture, drama with vivid writing and great characters.

IV

The Dick Van Dyke Show
"Baby Fat"

and

The Andy Griffith Show
"Man in a Hurry"

In the chapter on *The Phil Silvers Show* and *McHale's Navy*, I describe both as examples of "farce." With *The Dick Van Dyke Show* and *The Andy Griffith Show*, we move into the realm of "comedy." The distinction is worth exploring.

"Farce" is dominated by plot twists, physical humor, and simplistic wordplay, and its emphasis is purely on laughter. We have little investment in the welfare of the characters, because we know that ultimately no harm can befall them. In a sense, farces are cartoons involving human beings.

For instance, when watch the Three Stooges, we don't worry about the outcome of whatever story is at hand. We simply revel in the silliness. When Moe hits Curly over the head with a hammer, we don't ponder Moe's motivation or Curly's feelings. When Curly strikes back by poking Moe in the eyes, we don't contemplate the implications of sight imagery. No matter what we see or hear, any pain is temporary, and the horseplay will continue. In a way, farce is an enormous comfort, because we observe it without fear of consequence.

WALKING DISTANCE

To be sure, some farce is brilliant and inventive. Think about the Marx Brothers, or Laurel and Hardy, or even Abbott and Costello. Consider the plays of Feydaux and Sardou, or the most brilliant stage example from recent times, Michael Frayn's *Noises Off*. As we watch these works, we can't guarantee the outcome, but we are confident that the resolution will be happy, so we laugh without worry.

Not so with "comedy." In this dramatic form, the emphasis is on character. Thus in the richest examples we not only laugh; we also think and feel.

For proof we move once again to the works of Shakespeare. Near the end of *A Midsummer Night's Dream*, for instance, the so-called Mechanicals, led by Bottom, perform their version of "Pyramis and Thisbe." This scene may be the most surefire laugh-getter ever created. Right in the middle, however, Bottom, enacting Pyramis, begins to mourn his dead love, and at that moment his emotions, awkwardly phrased as they may be, become dramatic. The response from the onlookers onstage is epitomized by the words of Queen Hippolyta: "Beshrew my heart, but I pity the man" (V, i, 290). Meanwhile throughout the theatre, what merely seconds before was riotous laughter turns to silence. No matter how preposterous these men are, something within them and their performance touches us.

We can point to modern comedies for the same effect. In many of the films of Woody Allen, especially those in which he takes a part, we laugh at the romantic entanglements. Yet we are also involved in these relationships. At the end of *Annie Hall*, for example, Allen as Alvy Singer and Annie (Diane Keaton) meet outside a movie theater. We don't hear what they say, but in assessing their relationship, indeed, almost all relationships, Alvy conclude his narration with a joke about a guy who goes to a psychiatrist:

> "Doc, uh, my brother's crazy. He thinks he's a chicken." And, uh, the doctor says, "Well, then why don't you turn him in?" And the guy says, "I would, but I need the eggs." Well, I guess that's pretty much how I feel about relationships. You know, they're totally irrational and crazy and absurd, and . . . but I guess we keep goin' through it because, uh, most of us need the eggs (Allen 105).

The conclusion is funny and touching: comedy at its best.

Which brings me to the pair of shows under consideration here. Both were built around real people who confronted real but funny circumstances. Jokes were not the source of laughter. True, the characters on *The Dick Van Dyke* spouted plenty of one-liners, but the series centered on comedy writers. Moreover, the rest of the cast functioned in that milieu, where people usually talk in gag lines. Andy Griffith, on the other, often explained that his show had virtually no jokes *per se*. Indeed, when someone found in a script what might be considered a "joke," the line was probably removed. Physical comedy was certainly part of the show, especially when performed by the brilliant Don Knotts as Barney Fife, but he could just as easily be a figure who evoked compassion.

I should make one another point about why I've chosen to analyze these two shows in conjunction. Although they ran on network television during the same years, they existed at the antipodes of the social sphere. *The Dick Van Dyke Show* dramatized the life of a television comedy writer who worked in Manhattan and commuted from New Rochelle. Thus he moved between an urban and a suburban existence, and his life in both arenas was complicated by issues and egos attendant to the entertainment industry. The tone was as sophisticated as network television permitted at that time. *The Andy Griffith Show*, on the other hand, was set in a small North Carolina town, where homespun values and traditions held sway. Even though the show featured contemporary devices such as telephones and televisions, the pervasive feel was from decades earlier. As Griffith himself often clarified, the spirit of the series reflected the 1930s, not the 1960s. What both shows offered, however, was a devotion to realism. The characters behaved like "real people," and one measure of the affection and respect that these two series garnered during their day is how much "real people" still treasure them.

The Dick Van Dyke Show was created by Carl Reiner, who throughout the 1950s worked as a writer and performer for Sid Caesar on the acclaimed *Your Show of Shows* and *Caesar's Hour*. Using his own career and home life as a springboard, Reiner wrote a pilot and a dozen episodes of a show he called *Head of the Family*, about a writer on a television variety program who, like Reiner, lived with his wife and son in New Rochelle. The pilot was shot in 1958 but failed to sell. Nevertheless, Reiner's agent passed the script to Sheldon Leonard, another client, who recognized the concept's potential. Leonard had enjoyed a solid career in movies as a quintessential tough guy, but by now had moved to the other side of the camera and most recently served as producer and director of the successful comedy series *Make Room for Daddy*, also known as *The Danny Thomas Show*. Leonard's most important suggestion was that Reiner himself was wrong for the leading part of Rob Petrie, and proposed an actor then starring on Broadway in

Bye, Bye, Birdie, Dick Van Dyke. In response, Reiner modestly and wisely stepped aside to assume responsibilities for writing and producing. A side note: the other performer up for the part of Rob was Johnny Carson, then the emcee of the daytime quiz show *Who Do You Trust?* Imagine how different the history of television would have been had the future host of the *Tonight Show* been chosen instead.

Like his character is the series, Dick Van Dyke was raised in Danville, Illinois. After enlisting in the Air Corps and performing during World War II with Special Services, he worked as a DJ back in Danville, then toured with a partner in a comedy team called "The Merry Mutes." He began working in television in New Orleans as an emcee, and later appeared as a guest star on *The Phil Silvers Show* as a baseball phenom who as a Southerner is reluctant to pitch for the New York *Yankees*. For a time Van Dyke was anchorman for the CBS morning show, when Walter Cronkite was the newsman. But Van Dyke's big break was in the aforementioned *Bye, Bye Birdie*. After he was offered the lead role of Albert Peterson, Van Dyke protested that he couldn't dance as the part required, but director Gower Champion promised to teach him, and dancing soon became a Van Dyke specialty that he often demonstrated on his own series.

Next to be cast were the other members of the writing staff of the fictional "Alan Brady Show." Leonard already wanted Rose Marie to play Sally Rogers, a marriage-hungry show business veteran modeled on two women who at different times had been members of Sid Caesar's team: Selma Diamond and Lucille Kallen. Rose Marie in turn suggested Morey Amsterdam to play Buddy Sorrell, a self-proclaimed human joke machine (which Amsterdam was). Richard Deacon was brought on as the show's producer and the star's brother-in-law, the supercilious Mel Cooley, and six-year-old Larry Matthews was assigned to play the Petrie son, Richie.

One role remained to be cast: that of Rob's wife. More than sixty women auditioned, but none seemed right. Then Danny Thomas remembered an actress "with three names" who had almost been cast to play his daughter years before, but who with her pert nose would never have been accepted as the offspring of a man famous for his large proboscis. That girl turned out to be Mary Tyler Moore, who had trained as a singer and dancer and heretofore had done a few commercials. She was best known, if that expression applies, as Sam, secretary to Richard Diamond, the private eye played by David Janssen. On that show, however, only her legs were seen, although her sexy voice was heard as well. At her agent's urging, a reluctant

The Dick Van Dyke Show and The Andy Griffith Show

Moore, who had been disappointed many times, auditioned for Reiner, who stopped her in the middle of the scene, led her to Leonard's office, and asked Moore to read again. Soon the part of Laura Petrie (originally "Laurie") was hers. Jerry Paris and Ann Morgan Guilbert completed the basic unit as the Petrie neighbors and best friends.

During its first season, the show earned strong reviews, but ratings were weak, and the cast was convinced that they would be cancelled. Sheldon Leonard, however, rallied support, and during summer re-runs the show found its audience. For the next four seasons it was a clear hit, honored with many nominations and awards until Carl Reiner decided to end it before anyone sensed a decline in quality.

That quality was evident from the very first show; yet I've always felt that in the early scripts something was missing. Perhaps Reiner tried too hard to make Rob Petrie's life as normal as possible. The way the stories were structured, the character happened to work in television, but otherwise his existence might have been that of someone in an insurance agency. Meanwhile Rob himself rarely exhibited any of the eccentricities typical of a creative person, especially one who wrote comedy for a living. He was too bland, too tame. He wasn't, for lack of a better word, sufficiently "goofy." Instead Reiner seemed deliberately to avoid the manic spirit endemic to the business he knew, and when we now watch the earliest shows, we feel that void. Meanwhile Rob's wife, Laura, whose maiden name was originally Meeker, then changed to Meehan, was exactly as her name suggested: "meek." Although Laura's background, like Mary Tyler Moore's, was that of a dancer, the character initially lacked the brittle worldliness that a professional performer would have.

Soon, though, the dialogue began to acquire an "edge." The lines flew faster; the banter, especially from Sally and Buddy, turned sharper; and the characters became more defined. Moreover, the scripts concluded without any moralizing that implied, "We're just folks like everyone else." They weren't, and that difference created much of the fun.

Before I move to my episode of choice, let me celebrate what I believe is the best moment of the first season. It comes near the conclusion of the closing show, after Rob cajoles his old boss, Happy Spangler, into joining the Alan Brady writing staff. At first Spangler, played by veteran actor and vaudevillian Jay C. Flippen, proves a hindrance rather than a help, but under Rob's urging the two men write a sketch in the form of a lecture about comedy. The resulting sequence, as performed by Van Dyke, is a triumph;

not only in that particular story but for the series as a whole, as the disquisition about "sophisticated" laughter give free rein to Van Dyke's gift for physical gags and facial expressions. The show also let viewers feel as if we were peeking into a world about which we heard and read much, but knew little.

The Van Dyke series alternated between crises at home and troubles at the office, specifically with the production of "The Alan Brady Show." I especially enjoyed glimpses backstage, so I'm sure no reader will be surprised that I'm fond of scripts that featured Carl Reiner as the egomaniacal Brady. With his brash voice and overbearing assurance that masked insecurity, Brady bullied everyone, but particularly the luckless Mel Cooley. No matter what Mel said, Alan cracked the same response: "Shut up, Mel!" During the earliest episodes, we only heard *about* Alan. Later we heard his voice screaming on the phone, and subsequently we saw him in person, but not from the front. Finally in the fourth season we met him directly, and from then on his every appearance was a gem. As quoted in Vince Waldron's volume *The Official Dick Van Dyke Show Book,* Reiner hesitated before taking the part, figuring that the public knew him as a second banana to Sid Caesar and would not believe him to be a star, but fortunately he reconsidered. Many viewers assumed that Reiner based his characterization of Brady on Caesar, an admittedly explosive personality, but a more likely model was Milton Berle or Jackie Gleason, unchallenged dictators who controlled every aspect of the programs on which they starred and in doing so terrified their employees. Still, as Reiner diplomatically noted, "The stars of *all* those early variety shows were crazy. And for legitimate reasons. They were on live every week. And it was terrifying. The stress made them crazy" (Waldron 250).

"Baby Fat" certainly confirms that judgment, for it shows Alan Brady at his most neurotic yet vulnerable. This episode, the penultimate show of the fourth season, is not as celebrated as a few others, but Carl Reiner and Dick Van Dyke confessed that seeing the show many years after it was filmed reminded them what a superb piece of writing and performing it is (Waldron 250). The script by Garry Marshall and Jerry Belson was based on Marshall's experience trying to punch up a script for a famous comedian working in summer stock. According to Belson, Marshall didn't suffer all the humiliations endured here by Rob Petrie, but the ludicrous circumstances were nonetheless memorable (Waldron 366).

That information is telling. At production meetings of the Van Dyke show, Reiner often asked members of the company to relate incidents from their own lives, because he wanted the program to have a basis in reality, not matter how outlandish that reality might be. Such a strategy differentiated this program from the other great husband-and-wife sitcom of the era, *I Love Lucy*. No one ever questioned the comic gifts of Lucille Ball, Desi Arnaz, and the rest of the cast, but fundamentally that show was farce. The situations were deliberately bizarre, as when Lucy worked on an assembly line packing chocolates, when she stomped grapes in Italy, when she found herself on an apartment ledge talking to TV's Superman, or when she and her friend Ethel Mertz stole the cement block with John Wayne's footprints from Grauman's Chinese Theatre. One of the few touching moments on *Lucy* occurs when she tries to tell her husband that she is pregnant, but he has no time to listen. When he finally learns the truth in front of an audience at his nightclub, his happiness seems genuine, and so is the joy of everyone onstage. One reason for the success of that moment was the dramatic revelation itself. Another, probably more important, reason was the universal knowledge that the pregnancy in the script paralleled Lucy's own in real life, and the affection between husband and wife, whatever their off-screen difficulties, is affecting.

Except for such rare moments, though, realism was not part of *I Love Lucy*. All that mattered to its creators was creating laughter, and they certainly succeeded. The antics were brilliant, and Lucille Ball's talents were limitless. *The Dick Van Dyke Show,* however, came from another direction.

The distinction may be observed further in how the two lead actresses delivered their signature lines. When Lucy said "Oh, Ricky," she did so in only one of two ways. One expressed exasperation that her husband refused to let her join his act or execute some other scheme of hers. The other variety of "Oh, Ricky" was heard when they reconciled.

Laura's "Oh, Rob," on the other hand, was invoked in many different contexts, each reflecting a different aspect of Laura's complex persona.

"Oh, Rob!" (angry) How could you do something so foolish?

"Oh, Rob!" (desperate) Boy, are we in trouble!

"Oh, Rob!" (lost) What an unfair world!

"Oh, Rob!" (tearful) I'm so sorry!

"Oh, Rob!" (guilty) I did something terrible.

"Oh, Rob!" (wistful) I wish matters had resolved differently.

"Oh, Rob!" (shock) How could you even consider such a possibility?

No doubt I could find others that Mary Tyler Moore developed over the five years of the series.

Now to "Baby Fat," directed by series semi-regular Jerry Paris and originally aired on April 21, 1965. It opens with the three writers of "The Alan Brady Show" entering the star's office. Buddy is, as usual, eating what looks like a donut, and in the true spirit of a comedy writer complains that the star's quarters are decorated better than theirs. Sally has a typical rejoinder: "The men's room is decorated better." This pattern is characteristic of comedy writers. They think in jokes, so Sally's delivery does not feel artificially imposed for the sake of a laugh. Instead the style represents *who they are*. Here Buddy considers Sally's line, then retorts, "How would you know?" That Sally is a woman does not spare her from a sharp retort, nor does Sally expect to be spared. As the audience laughs, she jabs back: "The window-washer told me!" Admittedly these lines and several afterwards aren't brilliant, especially when read rather than spoken, but they reflect the characters. Therefore even if we've never seen the show, we immediately understand these people. The economy of exposition is superb.

With the entrance of producer Mel Cooley, the dialogue becomes more acrimonious. Mel is surprised that all three writers are in the room: "Why are *they* here?" he says to Rob, the only one whose presence is required. Buddy shoots right back at his perennial target: "We were playing bridge, and we're just waiting for the dummy!" When Mel insists that his instructions were "clear," Buddy fixes on the subject to which he returns in virtually every episode, Mel's baldness: "The only thing that's clear is the top of your head." In response to these remarks, Richard Deacon's sour expression is not only priceless, but, again, believable. He is the embodiment of straitlaced authority, condemned to endure the follies of creative subordinates. Their obstreperousness is the burden he must bear so that he can profit from their talent.

Next Alan Brady enters, played, as noted, by Reiner. He, too, wonders why Buddy and Sally are present, and Mel manages the rare achievement of a completing sentence in Alan's presence by explaining that they're just leaving. After a few more jokes, they do; then Alan turns on Mel: "I wanted to see Rob. That is Rob. I am Alan. This is the door. Use it." The machine-gun pace is terrific.

When alone with Rob, Alan searches his office. Usually he brims with confidence, so to see him proceeding with such trepidation is fun: "Rob, you're the only one I can turn to." A moment later he ends the introductory segment: "I want you to save my life!" Like Rob, we are mystified, and cannot wait to hear about the crisis at hand. What a brilliant opening scene.

The Dick Van Dyke Show and The Andy Griffith Show

After the commercial break Alan explains his predicament: "There's a bomb in this office." Further clarification reveals that the "bomb" is a script called "Baby Fat" by Harper Worthington Yates, winner of the Pulitzer Prize for drama and obviously a name to be venerated. Alan has been invited to star in Yates's latest Broadway production, an honor so prestigious that Alan is weighing a startling gesture: "I'm thinking of not wearing my hair." That Carl Reiner was bald was no secret, but Alan Brady still fosters the illusion. That is, until the first episode of the next season, when Laura, as an excited contestant on a game show, falls prey to the wiles of a clever host and reveals that Alan wears his toupee around the house. That show, "Coast-to-Coast Big Mouth," remains perhaps the most celebrated of the Van Dyke series.

At this moment, though, Alan's condition is still a secret. He reflects that he's been told that great art doesn't need hair, a judgment Rob confirms: "Picasso was bald. So was Guy Kibbee." After both men laugh, Alan explains that such humor is lacking from the script, and begs Rob to fix it. Rob is reluctant, so Alan reads an excerpt: "You're a Machiavellionaire," then inquires what that sentence means. When Rob explains that Machiavelli was an Italian statesman reputed to be ruthless, Alan admits that although *they* might know, "Who's gonna tell the audience?" Rob acknowledges that the humor is "esoteric," but Alan doesn't care about that problem: "It's just too highbrow."

Let's pause to consider the number of culture references in this little section. Picasso is familiar, but Guy Kibbee was a character actor from the 30s and 40s, and although his face might be recognizable, his name is not. "Machiavelli" is hardly commonplace, and how many in a nationwide television audience would recognize the word "esoteric" and understand that one of its meanings is "highbrow"? In other words, this script writes up to its viewers. The authors assume a level of sophistication that does credit to the series.

When Rob continues to doubt that Yates will approve any help, Alan reaffirms his desperation: "You've got my guts in your hands." At this outlandish exaggeration, Rob consciously wipes his jacket. His expression suggests that the gesture is as much for his own amusement as to resist Alan's supplication, but Alan persists about how important the play is to him: "This can make me the toast of Broadway. Don't let me get burnt." The joke is so feeble that Rob winces, but Alan explains that the line is from the script. Here's another example of the sophistication of the writing. To create a bad joke, but one that the audience will recognize as bad, takes skill, and that Marshall and Belson can appeal to both the audience's sense of humor and appreciation of wordplay reflects well on them and their expectations of us.

Back in the writers' office, Sally and Buddy are intrigued by the "suspicious" envelope in the bookcase, so like mischievous children they plot how to peer inside. (We know it contains "Baby Fat.") At last Buddy pretends to demonstrate the remarkable workings of a clasp, and Sally urges him to flip it faster. Then he tosses it on the floor, but the envelope still stays fastened. They're about to open it when Rob enters and innocently asks how the envelope could have fallen from the bookcase to the middle of the room. The sight of two worldly adults regressing is funny, but again, believable. They want to be true to their own consciences as well as loyal to Rob, but curiosity gets the best of them.

At home Rob is working at his typewriter in the dining room when Laura opens the front door while barely remaining upright under a load of packages. Rob is too preoccupied to notice, so when she shouts that she wants a divorce, he responds, "In a minute." Laura maintains the illusion: "Shall I call a lawyer?" "No," replies Rob. "I'll do it." Suddenly he grasps that something else is happening. Presently as Rob plugs away on the script, Laura inquires about the ethics of his work: "When you wrote a play, I always thought I'd be able to say, 'Hey, there! My husband wrote a play. Now all I can say is . . . 'Hey there!'" Mary Tyler Moore delivers that line with a beautiful deadpan. Rob tries to explain the legitimacy of his project, as much to himself as to Laura, and mentions two well-known play doctors: Jack Doyle and Dave Murrows. The latter name sounds remarkably like "Abe Burrows," and at the mention of it the studio audience laughs. Burrows co-wrote the musical *Guys and Dolls* and won a Pulitzer Prize for the book of *How to Succeed in Business Without Really Trying*, but he was also known as topnotch fix-it man on numerous other shows. When Laura suggests that Rob is "hiding in a closet," he denies the accusation, noting that he's in his own living room, but the image stays with us.

Next Alan Brady calls, essentially ordering Rob to join him in Westport, Connecticut for rehearsals. Rob has no desire to go, but is at a loss for excuses, so he seizes the best one available: "My wife's making a sandwich." The feebleness of this line is delightful. With no way out, Rob dumps his papers into his briefcase, piling a sardine sandwich on top. When Laura volunteers to wrap it, Rob asks if she has provided onion or tomato. When she confesses that she hasn't, Rob has the perfect button for the scene: "How do you like that? I have to punch up my own sandwich!"

In Westport Alan rehearses his lines, but remains disenchanted: "I'm not taking off my hair for this show." When Rob arrives, Alan is terrified lest someone see this intruder, especially Yates, who soon knocks on the door. "Quick, into the closet!" Alan orders. Yates then enters with his German shepherd, Mr. Ben, whom Rob saw earlier, and who begins to scratch at the closet in which Rob hides. Yates (played by the unique character actor Strother Martin), seems to be a parody of Tennessee Williams, with his courtly Southern manners and gay demeanor. At this point we might wonder about "in the closet," a phrase which recurs throughout the script. I cannot say whether the metaphor was operative in the mid-1960s, but if it was, I had no idea what it meant. Yet I can't help wondering whether the writers knew what they were doing, especially with the presence of both Yates and another gay character soon to appear.

After Yates politely exits, leaving, in his words, "the artist with the privacy he so deserves," Alan attempts to retrieve Rob from the closet, and the two become stuck between sliding doors. Alan demands the rewrites, which Rob provides, but when one of Laura's sardines sticks to the page, Alan recoils: "It's kind of frightening to look at a joke and have it look back at you." Pleased with Rob's efforts, Alan laughs and pounds him on the shoulder, sending the remnants of the sandwich flying. Thus Rob's degradation builds, but always within the bounds of reality.

After the commercial, we return to Alan laughing at Rob's efforts, then promising to treat him "like a person"; in other words, no more time "in the closet." But just then the director, Lionel Dann (played by ubiquitous television character actor Sandy Kenyon), appears, and Alan attempts to push Rob inside once more. This time Rob stands his ground, and Alan is forced to introduce him as his tailor, "Vito Schneider" ("Schneider" is German for "tailor"). When the director criticizes lines in the script, Rob instinctively blurts out that those are "some of the best in play." Dann is puzzled that Alan's tailor has read it, so Alan desperately covers: "You're a tailor, so tail!" What follows is Rob's taking a bar of soap and drawing a succession of pointless lines. First he disfigures his own jacket, a copy of which Alan is supposedly buying, then marks up and down Alan's pants. When Lionel suggests that the coat looks skimpy, Rob reacts with barely controlled fury: "I won't tell you how to direct. You don't tell me how to alter a suit." And he returns to his inane doodling. Rob's outrage when someone questions his tailoring skills is brilliant. Whatever the form in which he works, he has an artist's pride. Seconds later, he takes special pleasure in agreeing with Lionel's criticism of apricot bows on the leading lady's dress. Dann then accepts "Vito's" counsel as the advice of "a real pro." Before Rob can assert himself further, however, Alan scurries away with the director, and in desperation Rob tears his own jacket.

His casual remark about fashion receives retribution when the play's costume designer bursts in: "Who's Vito Schnoder?" Rob is forced to admit that *he* is indeed "Vito Schneider," inspiring a tirade from the obviously gay "Buck Brown" (played by Richard Erdman, perhaps best known for his leading role in Billy Wilder's film *Stalag 17*). Brown's name is ironically rugged for an effeminate man, who boasts about his own credentials ("I've designed sixteen Broadway shows"), then challenges Rob's credentials: "Can you double-stitch?" When Rob apologizes, Brown settles himself: "I'm sorry I flared." At this admission, Rob's expression is one of confusion. How does one handle such temperament? Ironically, we witnessed a similar display from Rob just moments before. But Brown doesn't remain calm for long, and as he leaves in a huff, he adds bitterly, "Now they want me to make a sweater for Mr. Ben. Bow-wow!" These days some viewers might be offended by the character's attitude and mannerisms, but I can't see why. Brown is simply a perfectionist who resents intrusion by an amateur. As Lance Mannion suggests in his blog:

> The joke is on Rob, a show biz professional in his own right, for his being unable to stick up for himself because of the ridiculous position Alan's put him in and having to stand there, stammering an apology, as a fellow pro berates him and dismisses him as a philistine (Mannion).

Alan returns to report that Rob's new lines, which Alan claimed were his, have been enthusiastically received. Rob assumes that now he'll be introduced as himself, but Alan insists they're "stuck with the story," especially because the producer is coming backstage. When Rob refuses to return to the closet, he is forced to exit through the window. Humiliation complete.

Rob returns home in disarray. When he trips over his son's skateboard, tucked, as his wife later observes, *in the closet*, he awakens Laura, who steps out in a stunning black nightgown. Rob sheepishly asks if he woke her, and Laura, who over the course of the series acquired the wit typical of the rest of the cast, replies, "No, I was going to get up to see what all the noise was."

The Dick Van Dyke Show and *The Andy Griffith Show*

Here is the moment to note how sexy a show the Van Dyke series was. Mary Tyler Moore was only twenty-three when it began. Yet unlike many mature actresses these days, who remain "girls" for as long as possible, Moore was clearly a "woman," physically and emotionally. Moreover, as Van Dyke has himself affirmed many times, even though Rob and Laura slept in twin beds, they acted like a sexually adventurous pair, certainly more rambunctious than any other couple on television until that time. In addition, Laura's capri pants were the stuff of major controversy, because the network worried that she looked too alluring, but the argument that women no longer adorned themselves in dresses and pearls to do housework earned grudging acknowledgment, so as the series continued she wore pants regularly. Still, her enticing qualities were also exploited less directly. For example, in the episode "Never Bathe on Saturday," Rob and Laura check into a Manhattan hotel for a weekend getaway, but while she takes a bath, her toe becomes stuck in the faucet. Reiner has said that he pictured all of America fantasizing about Moore lying naked in the tub. "October Eve" is about a portrait for which Laura posed fully dressed, but in which the artist (played by Reiner) painted her nude. Again Reiner assumed the country would relish the thought of Moore so exposed.

In this scene in "Baby Fat," she looks terrific, and even a disgruntled Rob is compelled to admit as much. When she inquires what Alan did to him, Rob puts the matter simply: "He put me in his closet." He then delineates the insults he has endured, including being called "a rotten tailor." When Laura asks who made such a bizarre accusation, Rob answers with resentment, "Buck Brown." Laura is nonplussed: "The cowboy star?" Rob replies bitterly: "Hardly." He seems to be disparaging himself rather than Brown, who was merely trying to do his job.

When Rob goes to the kitchen for a glass of milk, he almost drinks without benefit of a glass, but Laura cautions him: "Not out of the bottle." The way she utters this line implies that here is something she often says, and we are reminded how a marriage develops patterns that recur over a lifetime. This kind of knowing touch adds realism to this scene, this particular show, and the series in general. Another such moment occurs when Laura broods that Alan Brady makes her so angry, but Rob insists that his boss does not warrant all the blame. In response, Laura asks, "How come we can never be mad together?" Rob's behavior in that moment again suggests a pattern. When Rob explains, Laura offers the question at the heart of what we have witnessed: "You better decide who you're mad at." Rob understands that she's right, and rallies all his evidence, then concludes that if he marches to Alan with that level of anger, Laura will be able to say, echoing an earlier line, "Hey, there! My husband's out of work!"

Back in Alan's office, Mr. Ben looms over Alan, who cowers in his chair: "You're either his friend or his lunch." When Yates reflects that Mr. Ben is all he has left "since Blossom passed away," the news throws Alan: "I didn't know you were married." Yates's explanation, however, is simple: "Blossom was Mr. Ben's wife." Here Yates's expression suggests surprise at Alan's naïveté.

When Rob bursts in, he reluctantly reaffirms Yates's order for three suits. "And a dinner jacket," Yates pipes up. Yates then goes to make a phone call, but can do so only after Alan throws an unseen Mel out of his own office: "Shut up, Mel." Rob tries to reassert himself, but to assuage this anger Alan tries insult: "You've been talking to your wife." Rob, however, ignores the attempt to diminish his feelings: "No, I've been talking to myself." As Rob rants about the play's deficiencies, Alan cautions him to withhold criticism in front of the dog: "He's smart, and he bites." Even so, Rob turns directly to Mr. Ben and states his case, to which Mr. Ben sadly yawns. Alan chimes in with a terrific line: "Rob, that's cruel. He's a widower." But Rob will not be deterred. He explains that a lot of writers have trouble with their first comedy and thus doctors like "Murrow" (Rob omits the "s") and "Doyle" are needed. Now Yates returns, and Rob finally stands up for himself: "I am finished being a tailor. I am a writer." At this declaration Yates overflows with admiration: "I told everyone I was a writer when I was nothing but a butcher boy!" Eventually Rob leaves Alan to explain the situation, but when Alan starts, Yates is confused: "Your . . . tailor has a suggestion about my play?" While Alan stumbles over his words, Mr. Ben growls menacingly, and Yates's order to "Heel!" keeps the other two men in hilarious terror.

In the epilogue, Rob reveals to Laura that his efforts have been for naught because Alan and Yates agreed to work with the legendary Dave Murrows. Laura, though, has comforting words: "Harper Worthington Yates called . . . He wants his dinner jacket by Tuesday." She continues to think and speak in the proper comedy spirit.

Many other episodes from the series warrant salutation. A number were set during Rob's Army days at Camp Crowder in Missouri, when Laura worked as a USO dancer at the same post. Thus we witnessed their initial meeting, courtship, and marriage, plus many of the trials they endured as a penniless young couple. We also saw them dance together, and they were a well-matched team whose favorite song, we learned, is "You Wonderful You," written by Warren, Brooks, and Chapin and performed most famously by Judy Garland and Gene Kelly in the movie *Summer Stock*.

In "Buddy Sorrell, Man and Boy," Buddy prepares for and performs his belated Bar Mitzvah. The episode takes us to the actual service, at which a cantor chants in Hebrew, a remarkable moment for a 60s sit-com. We might also note how the presence of two Jewish characters (Buddy and Alan) as series regulars was singular during that period. Also memorable was "The Sam Pomerantz Scandals," in which Rob performs in an extended skit as Stan Laurel, who was, as mentioned earlier, Van Dyke's comedy hero. "Big Max Calvada," brings Sheldon Leonard out of his producer's office. In the days of radio drama, Leonard (or rather his voice) achieved a measure of immortality when he inspired reputedly the longest laugh in the history of the medium by threatening the notoriously cheap character played by Jack Benny: "Your money or your life." In this television episode, as a syndicate big shot, Leonard strong-arms Rob, Sally, and Buddy into writing a comedy act for his hapless nephew. The set-up is especially funny, as the writers stammer helplessly at the sight and sound of the notorious figure before them, and the reality that he is played by their real-life producer provides an underlying layer of fun. "Calvada," by the way, was name of the show's production company, formed from the names of the four principals: Carl Reiner, Sheldon Leonard, Dick Van Dyke, and Danny Thomas.

Finally I'll mention the one episode that gave the network the most worry: "That's My Boy???" It's another script of reminiscence, this one set after Laura has given birth. When the couple arrives home with the baby, Rob becomes convinced that their child has been switched with that of a family named "Peters." Various coincidences cause his panic to escalate, until Mr. Peters calls to stop by. The moment of revelation is brilliant: when Rob opens the door, his face registers shock. Then he invites Mr. and Mrs. Peters to enter, and we see that they are African American. As the audience laughs and applauds longer and louder than they do for any moment in the series, Rob's face communicates humiliation, relief, and befuddlement.

Backstage, however, the story was not so benign. As Waldron relates, the sponsor was convinced that the resolution mocked the black couple, but after extensive negotiation by Sheldon Leonard, the scene was shot as written, and the reaction was so happily overwhelming that seconds of laughter had to be cut so the program could fit into its allotted time.

WALKING DISTANCE

What makes this episode, and by extension, the Van Dyke series so strong is the maturity of the writing and the performances. Even as the creators worked within the standards of their day, they created a realistic world that proved remarkably entertaining, and which remains as funny, sophisticated, and, yes, believable as anything produced on television during that time. Within a few years, the tradition of quality the show established was continued by Mary Tyler Moore, when she starred in the highly acclaimed series that bears her name.

Another product of the Danny Thomas/Sheldon Leonard conglomerate was *The Andy Griffith Show*. It originated on February 15, 1960 as an episode of *The Danny Thomas Show*, in which Danny Williams (Thomas) is stopped by a North Carolina sheriff named Andy Taylor (Griffith) for passing a hidden stop sign. When Williams refuses to pay the fine, he must spend time in the local jail, which has all the comforts of a small hotel. Although Andy seems to be an archetypal bumpkin, he demonstrates wisdom and an essential goodness, especially when dealing with a variety of local characters, including his son, Opie (Ronny Howard).

Griffith himself first gained notice as a monologist, and in 1953 released his classic piece "What It Was, Was Football," told from the viewpoint of a country figure trying to understand a local game. His first important acting success was in 1955 in the television version of *No Time for Sergeants* on *The United States Steel Hour*. Griffith played the naïve Georgia boy Will Stockdale, who was drafted into the Air Force. The script was expanded for the Broadway stage, then for the movies, and each time its star won plaudits. During the movie, Griffith worked in one scene with Don Knotts, who became a lifelong friend and colleague.

The premise of the television series was simple. Andy Taylor was the Sheriff of Mayberry, a small town in North Carolina, modeled on Griffith's home town of Mount Airy, NC. Andy was a widower with a young son, and both men were cared for by Andy's Aunt Bea (pronounced "Ain't" Bea and played by Frances Bavier). For the first five years of the show, Barney Fife (Knotts) was Andy's deputy: officious and clumsy, but well-meaning and devoted to "Anj" and the town. Surrounding this core of characters were townspeople like Floyd the barber (Howard McNear), service station attendants Gomer Pyle (Jim Nabors before his singing career took off) and his cousin Goober (George Lindsey), and the town drunkard Otis Campbell (Hal Smith). Occasional guests included state officials and assorted criminals who tested the skills of the Mayberry police contingent, as well as mountain folk like the maniacal, rock-throwing Ernest T. Bass (*Your Show of Shows* alumnus Howard Morris, who also directed several episodes) and the superstitious but musical Darling family (led by veteran character actor Denver Pyle). Whenever they appeared, Griffith indulged his love of music and joined them in song.

When the series began, Andy Taylor played his part as a wily country boy, with a thick accent and a perpetual grin, a smarter relation of Will Stockdale. But according to producer Aaron Rueben, Griffith underwent an epiphany: "'I'm the straight man. I'm playing straight to all these kooks around me.'" (Kelly 41). Ruben describes Griffith's character from that point on as "Lincolnesque," the solver of everyone else's problems.

If one word may be said to encapsulate the key to the program's success, that word would be "respect," for Andy Taylor accorded all characters their rightful place. No matter their status, no matter how poor or rich they might be, no matter their problems or peculiarities, until a citizen or visitor created trouble, and even afterwards, Andy treated them with dignity.

With Barney, who was forever trying to make himself and his position in life seem more high-powered than they were, Andy had to exert control without crushing his spirit. Thus Barney carried a gun, but according to Andy's directive kept his one bullet in a shirt pocket. Plus whenever Barney made a fool of himself, Andy needed to salvage Barney's ego without letting Barney know. Every so often Barney faced the truth that he had puffed himself too full of hot air, and those realizations were invariably touching. For instance, in "Andy on Trial," Barney blusters carelessly to a woman reporter assigned to investigate Andy, who gave her editor a ticket. At the resulting trial, though, a humbled Barney speaks touchingly about the way Andy helps the citizens of Mayberry: "You gotta understand. This is a small town. The Sheriff is more than just a sheriff. He's a friend . . . when you're lawman and you're dealing with people, you do a whole lot better if you go not so much by the book but by the heart." Immediately the charges are dismissed. In the Epilogue, naturally, Barney boasts about how he brilliant he was, and Andy teaches Barney one more lesson.

With his son, Andy had to be both mother and father, and thus exert parental authority with a combination of firmness and compassion. What the relationship happily lacked was artificial patter. At times Opie reacted humorously, but the father-son bond was built on respect and love, and remained free from the wisecracks endemic to lesser series.

Despite his wisdom in dealing with Aunt Bea and the rest of the community, Andy did blunder from time to time, notably in his relationships with women. In "The Perfect Female," for instance, a cousin of Barney's girlfriend, Thelma Lou (Betty Lynn), visits Mayberry, and Andy highhandedly implies that she must meet his standard. When she defeats him in a shooting match, he learns from his mistake. Over the years of the series, Andy had relationships with several women, almost all of whom quickly departed. Griffith acknowledged that he and his writers had trouble writing for women, and only when he developed a friendship with Helen Crump, Opie's teacher (played by Anita Corsaut), did that side of his life become stable.

Perhaps the most important point to remember in appreciating any aspect of this series is that Griffith controlled all aspects. He supervised every script, and his values dominated every show.

No single episode reflects those values better than "Man in a Hurry," and no single episode better dramatizes what remains so appealing about the Mayberry way of life. The script was written by frequent contributors James Fritzell and Everett Greenbaum, and directed by Bob Sweeney, who helmed several dozen Griffith shows. This one first aired on January 14, 1963.

After the beguiling whistling theme song, the story begins with a car driving along a country road, then stalling. The driver, whose dark suit sets him apart as a stranger, steps out of the car, looks about in confusion, and sees a nearby sign that reads "Mayberry: 2 Miles." With no other option, he trudges toward the town, which he finds deserted. We then move to the church, where the community has gathered for services. As the congregation departs, Andy and Barney exchange pleasantries with the preacher, who notes that during the sermon Barney was dozing. Andy hurriedly explains that the previous night Barney had been up until four on a stakeout for chicken thieves, and the preacher is embarrassed to confess that he'll be having dinner with the suspects. Barney announces that he intends to head over to Thelma Lou's, but takes Andy aside to request a loan of fifty cents to buy a paper and some frozen bars. Finally Andy and Aunt Bea gather up Opie, who has been pulling horsehairs from his suit and now trades with his friend Johnny Paul. At this point the stranger, Malcolm Tucker, introduces himself to Andy, who of course greets him respectfully.

These details have nothing to do with the rest of the episode. In fact, if the same scene were presented as part of the script of another program, a story editor would probably cross out every action and line until Mr. Tucker greets the Sheriff. But this preliminary material is in fact valuable, for it establishes the rhythm of life in Mayberry. Such polite, seemingly trivial, exchanges may not propel anyone or anything forward, but they are intrinsic to this world. Mr. Tucker, we should note, is played by the wonderful actor Robert Emhardt, who appeared on television regularly throughout the 50s and 60s, often playing a corrupt businessman.

Mr. Tucker (as everyone calls him) urges Andy to head to the filling station, where surely someone will be able to fix the car. Andy cautions that the only one on duty is Gomer Pyle, but Mr. Tucker is confident that as long as the station is open, someone will be able to complete repairs. Andy is not so confident: "I wouldn't count on it."

At the filling station, Gomer suggests the problem might be lack of gas: "Sometimes when it says F, it's really an E." Gomer further explains that "F" stands for "Full" and "E" for "Empty." Mr. Tucker, a big-city gent, impatiently affirms that he knows the distinction. Andy then suggests that the only one who can service the car is Wally, so once again Mr. Tucker expresses his resolve. As they leave, Gomer cheerfully calls out, "Lotsa luck to you and yours," but Mr. Tucker is unmoved by the sentiment: "Why do they leave a boy like that in charge?" Andy has a simple answer: "It's just a part-time job. He's savin' up money for college. Gonna be a doctor." Andy delivers this line without the slightest irony. Gomer has ambition, and Andy sees no reason why it should not be fulfilled. We should mention that this appearance was the first by Nabors as Gomer. The character stayed with the show for a year, then branched off into his own show, *Gomer Pyle, USMC*.

The next stop is Wally's home, where after a few minutes spent ascertaining what specific sounds Mr. Tucker's car is making, Wally (Norman Leavitt) diagnoses the problem: a clogged fuel line. It requires only an hour's work, and he'll be glad to get right to it: tomorrow morning. Mr. Tucker is outraged, so Andy tries to comfort him: "If it were a real emergency . . ." To which Mr. Tucker assures him it is, because he has to reach Charlotte that night. Interestingly, Mr. Tucker never specifies why he's desperate to get to Charlotte. We assume he has a business meeting, but the details don't matter. Besides, Wally is more concerned with the contents of his newspaper: "Hey, did you see Moon Mullins yet, Andy?"

When Wally proves a dead end, Mr. Tucker returns to Gomer, and tries desperately to explain that because Wally has pinpointed the problem ("He's a wonderful man," gushes Gomer), surely Gomer can carry out the limited mechanics involved. Gomer rejects that possibility, but after cogitation remembers someone else who might help: his cousin, Goober. Mr.

WALKING DISTANCE

Tucker is elated but only briefly, because Gomer sadly adds that Goober spends every Sunday on his boat.

With no alternative, Mr. Tucker steals Gomer's truck, a theft that lands him in Andy's office, where, given the circumstances, the Sheriff does not press charges. Instead he invites Mr. Tucker home: ". . . before you get into any more trouble." The warning reduces Mr. Tucker to the level of a mischievous little boy. When the prisoner wants to make his one phone call, Andy explains that Mr. Tucker is not under arrest and can make all the calls he wants. But Andy adds one caution: the line will be tied up by the Mendlebright sisters, who live in different cities and by common consent are allowed to chat for hours every Sunday afternoon. This predicament sounds fanciful, even for Mayberry, which ought to have more than one phone line, even in the 1930s, but this episode exists in a unique universe, so let's not to question Andy's claim.

Mr. Tucker does, however, and back at Andy's house picks up the phone and overhears the sisters' conversation, to which he reacts with scorn: "This is ridiculous! Wasting valuable time on drivel—talking about people's feet falling asleep." Barney, though, is interested: "I wonder what causes that . . . I have that every now and then. I ought to see their doctor." The meandering thought is characteristic of Mayberry's citizenry. The more intriguing matter is Mrs. Tucker's use of the word "valuable." We don't want to ponder specific language to excess, but to what exactly is Mr. Tucker referring when he mentions something more "valuable" than two sisters comforting each other?

The Taylor family and Barney sit down to eat, but hungry as he is, Tucker declines all food. He tries the phone again, but once more is thwarted, even after he interrupts the ladies and tries to clarify his dilemma. When he hangs up in frustration, he utters one of the central statements of the entire series: "You people are living in another world!" So they are.

The scene moves to the porch, where we are treated to one of the most winning moments in television history. Andy sits with his guitar and begins to sing "The Church in the Wildwood," and seconds later Barney joins in harmony. As Mr. Tucker stands nearby, he lights a cigarette and begins to puff furiously, but gradually does so more gently. His brusque manner softens, and, almost unaware of himself, he joins in. Observing his reaction, Andy and Barney merely smile and continue to sing. The charm is irresistible.

In Neal Brower's book *Mayberry 101*, the author recalls showing this episode to a church group, and notes that when Andy and Barney sang "The Church in the Wildwood," voices from the congregation joined them until almost everyone shared the moment, just like Mr. Tucker (Brower 94-95). Brower also notes that "Man in a Hurry" was voted the favorite show from the series by members of the TAGSRWC (*The Andy Griffith Show* Rerun Watchers Club). Yes, such an organization exists and flourishes.

The tranquility is interrupted by Gomer's high-pitched voice, bringing news that Goober and he have towed Mr. Tucker's car and that Goober has started to work on it. At this report, Mr. Tucker becomes energized, and briskly sends Gomer on his way. Andy regretfully notes that Tucker is all keyed up again, a charge Tucker denies while pacing fiercely: "I'm not keyed up!"

What follows is a delightful sequence. Barney announces his plan for the afternoon: "Go home, take a nap, then go over to Thelma Lou's for TV. That's the plan." Between pauses, he slowly repeats this scheme three times, until Mr. Tucker can no longer bear to listen: "For the love of Mike, do it, do it! Just do it! Go home! Take a nap! Go over to Thelma Lou's for TV! Just do it!" All the while he strides across the porch. The scene contains nothing even resembling a joke, but hearing Tucker delineate the details of Barney's life is hilarious.

After Barney leaves, Mr. Tucker waits ever more anxiously. Andy tries to soothe him by asking whether Mr. Tucker has ever peeled an apple without breaking the peel, but the guest dismisses the thought. Even when Andy demonstrates that very act, Tucker is unimpressed: "Congratulations!" Once more Gomer returns, this time with a bulletin: Tucker's car needs sparkplugs. Tucker agrees to the purchase, but to make sure, Gomer reviews the price: "Eight cylinders, eight plugs." Once more Tucker agrees with urgency, so Gomer heads off. First, though, he stops, turns, and waves to Andy: "Goober says 'Hey,'" to which Andy naturally replies in kind: "'Hey' to Goober."

Finally Gomer drives up with the car, and Mr. Tucker hurriedly pulls out his billfold, but Gomer rejects the offer of money. No charge, he explains. It was an honor to work on such a fine vehicle. Tucker is incredulous, but Gomer resists. He does make one shamefaced confession, though: he took Goober's picture near the open engine.

Amazed at Gomer's attitude, Mr. Tucker walks slowly to his car. Aunt Bea is disappointed but hurriedly brings him a couple of chicken legs and a piece of cake, all "homemade, so they're better than you'll get on the road." Opie, too, has regrets: "If you were staying, I was going to sleep on the ironing board between two chairs . . . That's adventure sleepin'." This last line delights many viewers, but I've always felt it sounded artificial, an adult's idea of something cute that a child might say. I'm in the minority, however, and even if I'm right, a thirty-minute show is entitled to one false move. Opie then hands to Mr. Tucker the crushed penny for which Opie negotiated earlier: "It'll protect you in your travelin'." The last to wave good-bye is Gomer.

Mr. Tucker turns on the engine, which seems to purr, but for a moment he sits motionless behind the wheel. He looks at the group in front of him, then deliberates. Suddenly he exits the car and barks that the engine doesn't sound right. Gomer doesn't understand, but Mr. Tucker insists: "You and Goober did a fine job getting it started, but listen to that motor." Here he looks expectantly at Andy. "Don't you think I should wait until morning and let Wally look at it?"

As the camera focuses on Andy, he pauses, but quickly grasps Mr. Tucker's implication. He listens to the engine, then agrees that he wouldn't trust it for the highway, and that Tucker really should stay the night. Opie is delighted, as is Aunt Bee. A bemused Gomer confesses, "I just put in the gas" and starts to drive back to the station. First, however, Andy offers a final word of parting: "Lotsa luck to you and yours."

In the Epilogue, with the camera behind Mr. Tucker, Andy and Barney again sing, and when they finish, Andy suggests they go "uptown for a bottle of pop." Barney weighs this notion, and Andy repeats it, but this time Mr. Tucker is not infuriated. Andy wonders whether Mr. Tucker would like to join them, but he does not reply. Andy then confirms the plan, which Barney has already forgotten, and off they go. The final shot is of Mr. Tucker dozing, with a partially peeled apple in his hand and the peel unbroken.

Such a subdued ending was characteristic of the series. Another very popular episode that also ends quietly is "Opie the Birdman," written by Harvey Bullock. Here Opie is given a slingshot and warned to be careful, but he accidentally kills a mother bird. He doesn't admit his crime, but when the dead creature is found, and Opie remains inconsolable, Andy realizes what has happened. Instead of imposing direct punishment, though, he lets Opie listen to the baby birds calling for their mother, who will never return. That Opie himself lost his mother gives this scene genuine power. To compensate, Opie nurtures the birds until they are grown, but eventually must let them go. As they fly away, he mourns that their cage seems empty. Andy, however, offers the perfect reply: "But don't the trees seem nice and full." Here's a thirty-minute show, full of incidental humor, but which nonetheless dramatizes the cycle of life and death from the point of view of a little boy. Quite an achievement.

I'll mention one anomalous episode from the series. In "The Prisoner of Love," also written by Harvey Bullock, the state police ask to leave a suspected jewel thief in the Mayberry jail overnight custody. To the surprise of Andy and Barney, the prisoner turns out to be a stunning blonde (Susan Oliver), whom Andy ends up guarding. In response to his request as to whether she needs anything, she asks in a mock Southern accent, "Well, if it ain't agin' regulations . . ." (here Andy smiles shyly), could they talk? Andy obliges, and the next shot is of the prisoner's stocking feet dangling through the cell door bars, toes flexing playfully. At first Andy seems immune to her charm, but as the conversation grows more intimate, Andy enters her cell to help open her case. They stand so close that he is tempted to kiss her, but Barney interrupts, and a chastened Andy leaves, then returns later to find the prisoner nearly escaping. The next morning, Andy watches as the woman flirts with the arresting officers just as she as she did with him. Andy's reaction? "Well, you can't blame a girl for tryin'." Here the outside world invades Mayberry more sensuously than at any other time.

The Andy Griffith Show was the first in a succession of rural comedies produced by CBS, among them *The Beverly Hillbillies, Petticoat Junction,* and *Green Acres*. All ran for years, all made great profits, and all flourish these days in reruns. But these shows were fundamentally farces based on one overarching theme: most country folk are untutored and innocent yet somehow wise, while most city folk are educated and sophisticated yet somehow dumb. Episode after episode provided simple, even comforting, entertainment, but not one of these programs offered what the Griffith show did: an indelible touch of humanity.

At the end of the fifth season, Barney Fife departed Mayberry in what Don Knotts said was the most difficult decision of his career. He returned for occasional visits and additional Emmy awards, but while some of the new characters had charm, and ratings remained high, the magic started to fade. By the late 60s even Andy drifted out of many story lines until in 1968 the show was restructured without him as *Mayberry R.F.D.* It lasted three seasons.

After Knotts' departure *The Andy Griffith* was shot in color, and I suspect the effect of that change hurt as well. Like the New York and New Rochelle of *The Dick Van Dyke Show*, which never transferred to color, Mayberry was an illusory place, and the black and white world allowed us to escape the standards of realism that color demanded. Thus the Van Dyke shows offered what we imagined was the best of urban society: sophisticated and sexy. Meanwhile the Griffith show allowed us to escape into a small-town haven that featured the best of country existence: gentle and embracing.

Yet both shows achieved their end through similar means: sharply drawn characters who spoke believable dialogue and enjoyed relationships that sustained them through the pitfalls of life. That these pitfalls were often funny was a bonus.

These shows also reminded us that the richest comedy remains true to character, and lines that are funny when uttered by one figure in one situation would flop coming from a different character elsewhere. An insult from Buddy Sorrell wouldn't fit Barney Fife, nor would Gomer Pyle's "Lotsa luck to you and yours" be appropriate from any regular on *The Dick Van Dyke Show*.

Finally a word about the two stars. As different as their backgrounds were, and as contrasting as these men might seem in style and personality, Van Dyke and Griffith were great friends. From the time they met in New York City in the mid-1950s, their lives were remarkably parallel. Both achieved early success on Broadway, and both used that experience to springboard into a television series that bore their name and became a cultural landmark of the 1960s. After those series ended, both enjoyed some success in movies while also trying new ventures in television, but for a long time neither achieved the level of triumph they had experienced years before. Both underwent health problems: Van Dyke for alcoholism, Griffith for Guillain-Barré Syndrome. Both enjoyed comebacks late in life as good-humored but shrewd crime-solvers: Van Dyke as Dr. Mark Sloan in *Diagnosis: Murder*, Griffith in *Matlock*.

Even in these shows, however, their paths crossed. In the first episode of *Matlock*, Van Dyke played a judge who committed murder. Griffith's final role was in a two-part episode of *Diagnosis: Murder*, in which he recreated his role of Ben Matlock.

One other measure of their skills may be observed when we see them in parts that demanded different gifts. In an episode of *Columbo* called "Double Exposure," Van Dyke plays a photographer who engineers the murder of his wife, and he's as slimy as can be. To witness an even more terrifying portrait, watch Elia Kazan's 1957 movie *A Face in the Crowd*, with Griffith as "Lonesome" Rhodes, a savage hillbilly who uses the new medium of television to become a dangerous cultural force. Not only does the movie resound with today's nexus of politics and entertainment; after viewing it, you'll never look at Sheriff Taylor the same way.

Both works also confirm a truth about acting: if you want a first-rate dramatic performance, cast a comedian.

V

The Avengers
"Escape in Time"

and

Get Smart
"Casablanca"

In the Marx Brothers' 1933 classic *Duck Soup,* Chico and Harpo as Chicolini and Pinky briefly serve as double agents (sort of) for Ambassador Trentino of the fictional country of Sylvania. In an early scene, Chico and Harpo visit their boss's office, ostensibly to deliver information, but their efforts are interrupted by a ringing phone. As Harpo leaps to answer it, Chico warns a bewildered Trentino: "Shhh! This is spy stuff!"

The Avengers and *Get Smart* were all about "spy stuff. " Both were inspired by the character of James Bond, created in 1953 by Ian Fleming, who wrote a dozen novels and two short story collections that featured 007, the British agent notoriously "licensed to kill."

The 1962 film *Dr. No* made Bond an international sensation. I, too, became a fan, and during the summer of 1964, when I was supposed to be studying French several hours a day in school, I consumed the entire Fleming oeuvre of breezily nasty thrillers. The books as well as the films adapted from them demonstrated little concern for moral or political issues, but the movies were and continue to be more outlandish, with convoluted plots that feature mayhem, sex, gadgetry, and wit in roughly equal proportions.

That era also saw a plethora of other works about espionage. Some were sober portraits, such as John Le Carré's novel *The Spy Who Came in from the Cold* (1963), which in 1965 also became a successful movie. But irrespective of these serious exceptions, such a rich genre was ripe for parody and riffs, and among the best examples are the two shows under consideration here.

What *The Avengers* and *Get Smart* shared were preposterous stories and a sense of fun, qualities that made them required viewing for me. The most important of the many distinctions between them was their tone. *The Avengers* was coolly British, *Get Smart* broadly American.

Indeed, each seemed to embody its country's comic spirit, a contrast I understood only years after their initial broadcast. I was teaching at prep school, where one of my responsibilities was to supervise an afternoon tennis program. The assignment did not demand actual coaching; rather, with the help of a colleague, I coordinated the daily roster of student matches. During one semester, my partner was a visiting instructor from England, and the two of us spent many enjoyable afternoons chatting about Shakespeare and such. At the conclusion of each session, players were required to complete their exertions by running several times around the courts. When I took the lead, I directed our charges this way: "Okay, folks, time for your marathon." My colleague, however, phrased his command as follows (and please imagine these words delivered in a British accent): "All right, ladies and gentlemen, why don't you have at your little scamper?"

Here, I realized, was a key point. Much of American comedy is based on exaggeration, e.g., "The room was so small, the mice were hunchbacked." Much of British comedy is based on understatement, e.g., The Atlantic Ocean is "the Pond."

I relished both styles, and thus I enjoyed both shows.

My pleasure, however, was linked to another element they shared: each cast was led by a terrific male-female pairing. Even more important, both women members of the teams were impossibly alluring: Diana Rigg as Emma Peel on *The Avengers*, and Barbara Feldon as Agent 99 on *Get Smart*.

To *The Avengers* first.

Rigg joined *The Avengers* four years after the series started, when it had already undergone several transformations. At its start in 1961, it was not at all the program that would become world-famous. Instead it focused on Dr. Keel, played by Ian Hendry, a character very much like one Hendry had played in the show *Police Surgeon*. The premise of this new series was that after Keel's fiancée had been murdered, the doctor was inspired to investigate the myriad crimes he uncovered during his medical work. He was supported in this effort by a professional investigator named John Steed, played by Patrick Macnee, who had for a time abandoned his acting career to work as a producer in Canada, but had since returned to England. During the first season, though, Steed's whimsical professional attitude drew attention away from the grimly zealous Keel, and when the series shut down temporarily because of a strike, Hendry left to pursue a career in film. The show was then restructured around Macnee, who initially worked with three rotating partners. One, however, soon supplanted the others.

She was Dr. Cathy Gale, a widowed anthropologist who was also a judo master. As played by Honor Blackman, she changed the spirit of the show, as Macnee himself has written about Blackman and her successors, including Diana Rigg:

> All possessed enormous capacities of imagination, and knew how to take control no matter what the situation. They all played the role of women who were able to fight as well as seduce a man, and from which an aura of sensuality radiated, and this became the hallmark of the series. (Carrazé and Putheaud 13–14)

Gale was athletic and independent, and although sexual tension existed between her and Steed, their relationship never passed flirtation. Moreover, Gale resented Steed's authority and general disdain, so the two characters never enjoyed the personal warmth that would flourish between Steed and subsequent partners. Meanwhile Steed's responsibilities as a stalwart member of British intelligence became clarified, and he was also given a military background. Indeed, his entire demeanor changed, especially as regards his appearance. Instead of a traditional detective's trench coat, he wore tailored suits from Savile Row, complemented by a bowler (usually with hidden steel plate) and an umbrella (often with hidden sword). His effortless elegance and devotion to manners, in concert with his enjoyment of vintage automobiles and other traditional pleasures, transformed him into the image of the quintessential English gentleman from decades past. For her part, Gale was as modern as Steed was old-fashioned, and her passion for black leather and boots, as well as her physical daring, made her a sensation. But when Blackman was offered the role of Pussy Galore in the

James Bond film *Goldfinger*, she left the series, and the search began for a new partner.

After considerable experimentation, the new female character was given the name "Emma Peel," a shorted version of "M Appeal," or "Man Appeal." Dozens of actresses auditioned, and one was cast, but shortly after the first script was filmed, she was released. Finally a casting director suggested Rigg, a successful stage actress in her mid-twenties who had appeared with the Royal Shakespeare Company. She had never seen the show in any of its formats, but a test with Macnee revealed an obvious chemistry, and in 1965 the new team was unveiled.

Mrs. Peel, as Steed always called her, maintained much of the Cathy Gale tradition. She was beautiful and intelligent, as well as a master of hand-to-hand combat. Because her husband was assumed to have been lost flying over the Amazon, she and Steed were free to have an intimate relationship, but although the two often visited each other's homes, such a connection never developed.

That first season with Rigg was also the first done on film, and when the series initially ran in the United States, a new opening was included. It began with a human-sized chessboard, upon which a waiter holding a champagne bottle suddenly fell dead, a dagger driven into a target on his back. As Steed and Mrs. Peel walked to the body, the voiceover explained: "Extraordinary crimes against the people, and the state, have to be avenged by agents extraordinary. Two such people are John Steed, top professional, and his partner Emma Peel, talented amateur. Otherwise known as "The Avengers." Meanwhile Steed filled two glasses with champagne, and Emma replaced her gun in her boot. After the click glasses, they departed together.

Although added solely to help audiences understand the show's premise, this opening communicated key elements of the series. We had no idea for whom Steed and Mrs. Peel worked, nor whom they were trying to stop. We had no idea why the waiter was killed, nor in light of Steed's manner did we care. Finally, whatever Steed's profession, he would always have time to indulge his refined tastes and share them with his "partner," as Mrs. Peel was designated. She, in turn, carried a weapon she was clearly accustomed to wielding. Finally we could assume that the series would overflow with outsized villains, and, sure enough, we regularly met crackpot scientists and megalomaniacal criminals bent on world domination. The result was a growing emphasis on science-fiction elements, affectionately known as "spy-fi."

This trend would become even more pronounced in their next season, which was shot in color, thanks to an influx of money from American network television. By now the characters, their activities, and their relationship were so established that the explanatory prologue was eliminated. Yet the new opening maintained the same themes. As Steed prepared to open a bottle of champagne, Emma shot out the cork. Flashing his umbrella sword, Steed tossed Mrs. Peel a flower which she inserted into the buttonhole of his jacket. Then the two indulged in other amusements (or so we were invited to imagine).

What neither opening established was time or place. Rather all these scripts occurred in a vague universe that some commentators have called "*Avengers*land" (Cornell, Day, and Topping 129). Brian Clemens, associate producer, writer, and perhaps the key creative force behind the series, explained that "Ours was a fairy-tale world – the kind of Britain that outsiders like to imagine it is, even if is not" (Carrazé and Putheaud 129) He also noted that:

> There would be no extras *per se*—everyone on screen would be a character. This was because our main characters, as outrageous as they were, would look ridiculous if placed alongside real, documentary-like people . . . we never got involved in 'real' problems . . . (quoted in Carrazé and Putheaud 129)

Thus the program existed outside contemporary social turmoil. True, preoccupations of the day were sometimes worked into scripts, but always with a light touch. *The Avengers* thus stood with one foot in reality and the other in fantasy. Clemens also insisted that in the course of the shows "no woman would be killed (although they could be bound, gagged, and generally debased!)" (Carrazé and Putheaud 129). The result was a bizarre sexiness spiced with wit and a healthy dose of British eccentricity. But what ultimately carried each episode was the insouciant charm of the actors in combination with the playfulness of the stories, which in their own way mocked not only traditional dramatic convention but their own reliance on such convention.

A good example of these elements working in unison is a show from Rigg's second season called "Escape in Time," written by regular contributor Philip Levene and directed by John Krish. It was filmed in 1966, but first broadcast in America on July 17, 1968.

As the program opens, one of Steed's colleagues, whom we later learn is named Clive Paxton, snoops around a country home. At the center of a large room stands a collection of busts resting on a pedestal, and all are variations of one head and face. As Paxton walks through a double door, he feels himself falling. He wakes up in the same house, but with older furnishings, at which point a man in Elizabethan dress appears and shoots him.

Here is a specific example of the general form that characterized the beginning of many episodes: an inexplicable occurrence leaves us wondering about the significance of what we have seen. The title of the show flashes next, followed by two explanatory subtitles: "Steed visits the barber; Emma has a close shave." In other words, we're being taken for a ride, and nothing we are about to see need be regarded seriously.

We next move to Mrs. Peel's home, furnished with contemporary accoutrements. Thus the contrast between her and Steed is confirmed. Everything about Steed, from his cars to his living arrangements, suggests a man maintaining the values of a distant era. Mrs. Peel, on the other hand, embodies the "mod" spirit that took hold of England during the 60s. Such is especially the case with her apparel. Between the first and second seasons, Rigg strongly requested that her wardrobe be changed from the black suits she had inherited from her predecessor, and therefore her personal designer was hired create a series of jumpsuits in bright colors, soon to be called "Emmapeelers."

In this scene Mrs. Peel is dressing elegantly in response to an invitation to a "Grand Hunt Ball," but just as she is ready, Steed enters magically and flips the card. The other side reads: "We're needed." Here is the pattern in almost every show. Often we have no idea how Steed slips in either his message or himself, but the light touch works beautifully. Remember, we are in the realm of fantasy, where suspension of reality is intrinsic.

We move to a mortuary, where a Mr. Clapham explains that the body was fished out of the Thames at 3:45 AM, but that the more curious aspect of his death is the bullet that killed him. Mrs. Peel immediately identifies the weapon: a sixteenth-century gun of medium caliber, probably a sporting piece used exclusively by noblemen of the Elizabethan period. "Curiously archaic," she observes. "Ah!" interrupts Clapham, "but the problem is very up to date!" He speaks with an enthusiasm borne of mania, a familiar motif in the series. More important, can we think of another show where the woman demonstrates similar mastery of firearms? Admittedly, on some contemporary crime or spy shows women evince similar expertise, but they usually voice their knowledge as if daring a male colleague to protest that his manly prerogatives are being usurped. On such programs the characters maintain sharp demarcations between masculine and feminine responsibilities. Here, however, the self-assured Steed revels in Mrs. Peel's knowledge, so the male and the female can truly be colleagues and equals.

After Clapham explains that several criminals on the run have vanished, Steed and Mrs. Peel continue the discussion in Steed's apartment, a more classical dwelling than Mrs. Peel's. The two review the disappearance of other "evildoers," as Mrs. Peel blithely calls them, including one whose expression of avarice reminds Steed of "an auntie of mine." Another is a President named Bibi Gin, a name that inspires Steed to query, "I wonder what did happen to Bibi Jin?" The pun on the well-known Bette Davis–Joan Crawford movie returns us momentarily to the real world, but the dialogue throughout features repartee between two sophisticated people who genuinely enjoy each other's company.

The last face they see is another of Steed's cohorts, Tubby Vinson, who in the next scene visits that same mysterious house. He, too, walks through the double door, and this time we pay more attention to the special effects. They seem to be a burlesque of the psychedelic images that dominated pop culture during the 60s, a subtle commentary on the desire for all manners of "escape" that were prominent then. When Vinson awakens, he looks out the window and sees a man riding a white horse. That man then enters and stabs Vinson with a Jacobean knife. Though mortally wounded, Vinson manages to reach Steed's apartment with information that one of the "evildoers" will be at "Mackidockie Court." Naturally Steed and Mrs. Peel resolve to be present as well.

There they indeed find the escaped criminal, Colonel Josino, carrying a stuffed giraffe, of all things, who follows a complicated route through narrow winding streets that seem deliberately like a stage set. First Josino meets a woman named Vesta, who swaps his giraffe for a crocodile. Next he meets a vendor named Parker (played by gaudily jacketed Nicholas Smith, soon to star in the international television hit *Are You Being Served?*). Parker swaps the crocodile for a kangaroo, from which Josino takes a message, then eats it and moves on. Meanwhile Steed and Mrs. Peel follow closely, and each time Josino turns to see if anyone is trailing him, they embrace. As we observe this scene, we cannot help but think of all the television shows and movies that feature agents trying to plumb the hidden meanings in rituals carried out by subversive organizations. Here the plan and the setting are both laughable, as indicated by Steed's and Mrs. Peel's breezy attitude.

The Avengers and Get Smart

Ultimately Josino ends up in a barber shop run by "T. Sweeney," a playful reference to the notorious "Sweeney Todd," not yet the subject of a Sondheim musical, but still famous in his own right. When Josino emerges with a black cross on his cheek and a stuffed elephant, Steed tries to follow, but loses him among the other establishments hidden within these streets, including an Asian antique shop. Eventually Steed seems to discover him, but his prey turns out to be another man wearing Josino's outfit. Meanwhile Mrs. Peel follows Vesta on a drive into the English countryside. This long scene has no dialogue, but the music underneath bounces playfully, and the physical movements, especially the sudden embraces and releases, match the rhythm. In sum, by the conclusion of these two scenes, we have become immersed in *Avengers*land.

In hot pursuit, Mrs. Peel drives her appropriately modern and speedy vehicle, a Blue Lotus. Steed will later drive his classic Bentley, unsuitable for chases, but perfectly reflective of his style. Here Mrs. Peel finds the stuffed crocodile on the road, but when she stops to retrieve it, she is pursued by a man in equestrian habit on a motorcycle. Again, trying to maintain logic in this series is fruitless. After an elaborate chase, in which Mrs. Peel runs, jumps, and rolls across the area, she eludes him, the motorcycle explodes, and we find ourselves back in her apartment. Here, as she creates a stuffed giraffe for Steed to take on another tour of Mackidockie Court, Steed remarks that he never realized she had such a gift for sewing. "Our relationship hasn't been exactly domestic," she retorts. We, of course, wonder just what that enviable relationship entails, but ambiguity is endemic to its fascination.

Now Steed takes Mrs. Peel's giraffe, and as she follows, he enters the Mackiedockie maze. Almost dancing his way through, he visits the same barber, and emerges with the same taped cross and stuffed elephant. With Mrs. Peel playfully close behind, Steed enters the Asiatic emporium, where a young woman in a sari, who calls herself Anjali, removes the cross from his cheek. She explains that Steed will be protected by Ganesha, the elephant god who removes all obstacles, then inquires what price Steed would pay for escape. "Half my kingdom," says Steed with a smile that reveals his amusement. "Our terms exactly," replies Anjali. She confirms his height and weight, then tells him to follow orders. These convoluted directives again mock the countless spy movies in which similar instructions are dispensed with all seriousness. When Steed departs, Mrs. Peel attempts to stay close behind, but when she catches his figure, it is not Steed, but a menacing imposter. Mrs. Peel disposes of him with a few karate chops, but still remains uncertain of Steed's whereabouts.

Meanwhile he has been led into a funeral hearse where, with Verna holding a gun on him, he is blindfolded and taken to that house where earlier the two agents were attacked. Here Steed meets the prime mover of the story, Waldo Thyssen, a well-dressed eccentric whose stammer and unsettling glint insinuate that his geniality masks malevolence. He is played brilliantly by Peter Bowles, who later enjoyed great success on a number of British television programs. Thyssen claims that he can send people back in time, and for proof runs a brief movie of the famous racetrack Epsom Downs in 1904. "A little before my time," comments Steed. "Not necessarily," says Thyssen, as an astonished Steed sees on the screen the same Colonel Josino that he has sought. In the meantime, Emma stuffs another giraffe.

Thyssen next suggests a test run, inviting Steed to visit the year 1790. Steed anticipates a return to Waterloo, but Thyssen explains that the trip will cover time, not distance. Thus Steed will end up in the same house, which has been in Thyssen's family for centuries. Furthermore, the 1790s was the generation of Samuel Thyssen, a notorious philanderer, so Steed naturally approves of his company. After describing more of his celebrated descendants, Waldo recalls the first: Matthew, an inquisitor who was "said to have invented the rack." At once we realize that for this story to come full circle, someone must have a run-in with Matthew. After Steed changes into appropriate garb, Thyssen leads him to the familiar door, then works what is supposed to be a time device. It looks exactly like a slot machine, and a cheap one at that, so we would not be surprised to see it turn up fruits instead of the date that appears. Here is another instance when the series suggests that we take none of this adventure seriously.

Steed embarks on the customary journey and finds himself in the same room, but furnished in the style of the eighteenth century. We notice that only two of the several busts are in place. Outside, a carriage drives up, and a man and a woman jump out, then burst laughingly into the room where Steed has hidden. With the illusion complete, Steed follows the couple through the same door and ends up back in the present. Thyssen and Steed then make a deal for diamonds, and the scene ends before Steed is blindfolded and returned home.

Next Mrs. Peel takes her turn in Mackidockie Court. The members of the team are surprised to see her, and Anjali in the Asian shop mutters darkly that their "European agents" should have said something, but Mrs. Peel is nevertheless given directions. As she turns the corner, a wall opens, and she is pulled inside. Simultaneously Vesta, dressed exactly like Mrs. Peel, breaks through. She is about to walk away, when she suddenly realizes what has happened, but the wall has already closed behind her. As Mrs. Peel sits blindfolded in the hearse with Parker and Sweeney, the three fold their arms in unison, another directorial touch that mocks the very suspense that is supposed to be building.

Next Steed visits Mrs. Peel's apartment. He presses the doorbell elegantly with the tip of his umbrella, but when she doesn't answer, he lets himself in (first identifying himself by his bowler perched on his umbrella) and finds the raw materials for the stuffed animals. Grasping what Mrs. Peel has done, he dashes off to find her, and with Clapham driving, attempts to find the house in question. When Steed remembers that during his first trip (when he was blindfolded) he heard turkeys, Clapham identifies their destination.

Mrs. Peel, in turn, has now met Waldo Thyssen, who is ready to begin her trial run. But where to go? The question evokes clever wordplay involving "year" and "vintage." Mrs. Peel rejects Victorian times: "I hardly think they'd be amused." Then Waldo suggests the Georgian era, when women like Mrs. Peel were appreciated: "You n-n-need to be appreciated, Mrs. Peel." Mrs. Peel seems agreeable. "I appreciate . . . your appreciation." With every word from Mrs. Peel, Thyssen's stuttering becomes more pronounced. When, however, he proposes the Elizabethan period, Mrs. Peel declines: "The men were so . . . tiny." Her sexual implication is obvious and apparently sparks something inside Waldo, who expresses relief that she will not meet his forebear Matthew: "He was so cruel . . . especially to . . . p-p-p-pretty women." Thus they decide on the eighteenth century. And when should she leave? Thyssen offers the obvious answer: "There's no time like the p-p-p-present."

When Steed and Clapham find a Yuletide Turkey farm, Steed is confident they are close to the correct house. But Vesta has already arrived, just as Mrs. Peel, dressed in a magnificent Georgian gown and adorned with a beauty mark and a blond wig, steps inside the familiar door. Thyssen is about to "send her back" when Vesta shouts that Mrs. Peel was the woman who trailed Steed on his escape route. Waldo's solution is the one we expect: he will divert Mrs. Peel further back to meet the notorious Matthew. Taken with this thought, as reflected by a bit of psychotic giggling, he dials the slot machine to 1570, when Emma awakens. As she searches the room, appropriately furnished, she finds Josino's body in a trunk. In the background we see only one bust on the podium, but suddenly it comes to life, and Matthew steps out. Mrs. Peel tries to escape, but her path is blocked by a grinning and hooded torturer/executioner.

Steed and Clapham find the correct house, but it doesn't fulfill Steed's description, until he spies a plinth on a frame with Ganesha, the elephant god. The scene then switches to the torture chamber where Emma sits imprisoned in stocks, her bare feet protruding. Thyssen's dialogue here is wonderfully flavorful: "These strange clothes you wear! The devil's work! Designed to inflame a man's passion!" An amused Mrs. Peel warns him: "You should see me 400 years from now!" "Time" has been a motif throughout the episode, recurring in the form of proverbs and familiar phrases. Tearing off her wig, Thyssen raves: "You're a heretic! A bawd! A witch!" But Emma merely laughs: "I could think of some names to call you: short . . ." (we wonder whether she refers to those names or to Thyssen himself) "up-to-date, highly descriptive names." We are left to conceive what these words might be. Thyssen then elevates his threats: "We shall purge your secrets from you . . . you will recount every step of your journey." Emma dares him: "That will take some time." But Thyssen temporarily has the last word: "Time is something we have a-plenty."

The style of this scene is terrific. The setting is simple but atmospheric, Mrs. Peel looks glamorous, and Peter Bowles as Thyssen is genuinely malevolent. The artifice is obvious, but so cleverly maintained that we are absorbed.

As Steed approaches the house, he subdues one member of the team with gas from his umbrella tip, then once inside comes upon Vesta, who holds a gun to the back of his head and sneers that Mrs. Peel is with Matthew. Steed sums up his plight: "Mrs. Peel in the hands of the enemy; my confederate [Clapham] lying unconscious; a loaded gun pointed at my neck; I'm trapped." But immediately he spins and grabs the gun: "Shall we dance?" We are in the realm of meta-television (if such a form exists), as Steed mocks the melodramatic story in which he plays a part. Soon he ends the scene in ever-gracious style, leaving Vesta handcuffed around a pillar. The action then switches back and forth from Emma to Steed. As Thyssen's hooded aide heats a poker in the roaring blaze, Steed stylistically fights through a guardsman in the eighteenth-century room (while dancing a minuet with a lance), then past Parker wearing Elizabethan costume.

The Avengers and Get Smart

Just as the tools of torture are ready, Steed interrupts the session: "Well, how d'you do?" He releases Mrs. Peel, and the final battle is underway. With a few chops, Mrs. Peel conquers Thyssen, then fans herself while Steed, armed with that same lance, knocks out the executioner. Thyssen, however, recovers and stands holding a gun, prompting Steed to resume the central imagery of the teleplay: "You're a little ahead of your time, aren't you?" Thyssen tries a reposte: "Your time, Mr. Steed, is running out." Steed and Mrs. Peel then evaluate Thyssen's various roles: Steed enjoys Matthew ("much more in character"), but Emma prefers Samuel, "a loveable little rogue." She delights in ridiculing him. As Steed still holds the lance, Thyssen orders him to drop it, but Steed and Mrs. Peel merely turn the weapon on Thyssen and push him into the trunk.

After the two explain to each other (and us) the mechanics of "the time machine," they scurry back through each period room until they reach the 1960s. "And next stop the moon," says Steed, with prescience. Mrs. Peel comes across Vesta, still handcuffed to the pillar, and looks at Steed, puzzled: "Didn't we get the vote?"

The tag scene returns us to Ms. Peel's apartment, where Steed offers another escape route, this one to a party. Outside, somewhere, Steed ushers Mrs. Peel into the back seat of a vintage roadster, but it will not start, so with a tip of his bowler he allows Mrs. Peel to turn the ignition key while he peruses the back. Unfortunately the engine backfires, so Steed's face ends up sooty. Nonetheless, with yet one more tip of the bowler, he settles in the back seat, and Mrs. Peel drives them off to . . . ?

The plot convolutions of this episode make little sense. We never receive an explanation for all the peregrinations in Mackidockie Court, nor do we learn how Colonel Josino appears in a film from 1904 or why Thyssen requires a multi-person staff to conduct what is basically a one-man operation. But to ask such questions is to ignore the spirit of *The Avengers*. "Its focus on the bizarre and the improbable provides weightlessness to the principal characters, lifting them beyond the contingencies of time and place that mark out naturalism and realism" (Miller 129). That analysis may be a bit bombastic, but it does capture the essence of the show, which could also be found in the titles of episodes. "The Girl From Auntie" echoes the American series *The Man From UNCLE*, while "Mission: Highly . . . Improbable" obviously plays with *Mission: Impossible*. The American title clarifies its no-nonsense agenda, while the British version suggests that mature nonsense is the goal. "The Winged Avenger" is a takeoff on

Batman. Even within episodes, names of criminal organizations suggested a winking irony. "The Hidden Tiger" features an organization devoted to cats that bears the acronym "P.U.R.R.R.," and functions under the aegis of men named Cheshire, Angora, and Manx. In "The Correct Way to Kill," an institution dedicated to training bowler-wearing young men calls itself of "S.N.O.B." In "The Joker," in which Mrs. Peel is said to have recently published a book on bridge, a fellow expert on the game is called "Sir Cavalier Rousicana." And in "Who's Who," a stilt-making firm is labeled "Hi-Limba."

That last episode, also written by Philip Levene, deserves comment, for it offers a variety of amusements. The show's premise is that a scientist (mad, of course) has created a device that transplants "minds, souls [and] entire psyches" from one person to another, and Steed and Mrs. Peel are promptly swapped with two enemy agents, Basil and Lola. When the phony Steed greets the as yet un-switched Mrs. Peel, he calls her "Emma." Later, when both have been switched, Steed affectionately pats her bottom, and the two kiss. We are also treated to such unlikely sights as Mrs. Peel chewing gum and dancing to music of the 60s, while Steed's hair is mussed and curled with Brylcreem and his tie is pulled askew. After each commercial break, a deadpan British announcer reviews the plot with pictorial help, but then confesses that he himself does not understand it. Perhaps the best moment occurs when Mrs. Peel is switched back to her own body, but must convince the still disguised Steed of her identity. After she grips him in a headlock, she whispers something we cannot hear. Whatever she says, Steed is immediately convinced, and charmingly tries to recovery his dignity.

However whimsical the stories of *The Avengers* were, the heart of the series was the relationship between the two leading characters, a combination of affection and respect. Steed was enchanted by Mrs. Peel's intellect, imagination, skill, and courage, while she treasured his graciousness, wit, and intrepidity. Together they formed the most winning couple in the history of television.

After two seasons on *The Avengers*, Diana Rigg moved on, apparently for several reasons. According to reports, she was not happy with the production team and also disliked the onrush of fame. She also claimed that as an actress she needed to try new projects. Ironically, like Honor Blackman before her, she soon worked in a James Bond movie, *On Her Majesty's Secret Service*, in which she was the only woman ever to marry Bond, enacted this one time by George Lazenby. That Diana Rigg should have been part of such a disappointing entry has forever frustrated fans of both Bond and

The Avengers and Get Smart

Ms. Rigg, but thereafter she built a distinguished stage and television career, and incidentally remains good friends with Patrick Macnee.

When Rigg departed, and with Steed left as the fulcrum of the show, Linda Thorson was hired as the new female co-star, playing Tara King. The transition was carried out in the episode called "The Forget-Me-Knot," in which Ms. King is introduced by working with Steed on a case, but which also features the most touching moment in the *Avengers* canon. In the concluding tag, we see a newspaper headline: "Peter Peel Alive." Next we see Steed on the phone, requesting a new partner. Mrs. Peel arrives to reveal that her husband will pick her up shortly, then leans in to Steed and whispers: "Always keep your bowler on in times of stress –and a watchful eye open for diabolical masterminds!" After one more whisper, she turns to leave. Steed calls out "Emma," she looks back once more, and he says simply "Thanks." Heading off for the last time, Mrs. Peel passes Tara on the stairs, and advises that Steed likes his tea "stirred anti-clockwise." From his window Steed observes Mrs. Peel escorted to her car by a man dressed exactly like him. An amusing myth holds that Macnee played the role, but in the long shot, at least, Mr. Peel was actually enacted by the show's Stunt Coordinator.

The emotional impact of these moments was not limited to viewers. Macnee has confessed that after filming this scene, he went to his dressing room and cried.

The Tara King episodes in 1968–69 were not as successful. Thorson was significantly younger than Macnee, and despite her professional status in Steed's organization, we were never certain how competent she was meant to be, nor the nature of her relationship with Steed. The producers also tried to return to more realistic stories, but despite a few entertaining episodes, the new combination never captured the public's imagination, and in 1969 the series was discontinued.

It was revived as *The New Avengers* in 1975, with Steed playing more of a supervisor than a field operative, in charge of two younger agents: Gambit, played by Gareth Hunt, and Purdey, played by Joanna Lumley, who would achieve greater success in *Absolutely Fabulous*. Twenty-six episodes were produced, and they did run in the United States. No doubt I saw a few, but they made no impression on me. Nor did a 1998 filmed story featuring the same characters as played by Ralph Fiennes and Uma Thurman.

No matter. I can still enjoy Emma Peel and John Steed in their heyday, and no one can ask for more.

Yet I have more.

Get Smart was the result of a suggestion from Talent Associates partner Daniel Melnick that he made separately to Mel Brooks and Buck Henry. Brooks was not yet an acclaimed movie director, but was still well-known as a writer for Sid Caesar on *Your Show of Shows* and *Caesar's Hour*, while Henry had been a writer for Steve Allen and *That Was the Week That Was*. Speaking to each man, Melnick noted that the two most popular film franchises of that time (the early 60s) were James Bond and Inspector Clousseau, the bumbling French detective played by Peter Sellers in the "Pink Panther" movies. After Melnick suggested combining these characters on one television show, Brooks and Henry created a script with the thought that comedian Tom Poston might play the lead role of Maxwell Smart. ABC, however, passed on the project twice.

At the same time, NBC was seeking a vehicle for Don Adams. After discharge from the Marines in World War II, during which he almost died from illness, Adams had held many jobs, but was then working as a stand-up comic. Among his routines was an impression of William Powell, star of the "Thin Man" movies. That actor's clipped delivery, amplified with the former drill instructor's biting intonation, was unique, funny, and, perhaps most important, infectious.

One of Adams's childhood friends, Bill Dana, had become famous by impersonating his own creation "Jose Jimenez," a timid Puerto Rican figure whom in monologue Dana placed in many situations, most famously as an astronaut. When Dana was about to star in a series as "Jimenez" playing a hotel bellboy, he suggested to the producers that Adams should be added to the show as the house detective. Thus "Byron Glick" was born, an overconfident bumbler who would morph into Maxwell Smart.

As a side note, I'll add that the Dana series was a spinoff from *The Danny Thomas Show*, on which Dana as "Jimenez" appeared as an elevator operator. Moreover, as I've already mentioned, members of the Thomas production team helped create *The Dick Van Dyke Show*, while the Thomas show itself was the springboard for *The Andy Griffith Show*, which in turn inspired *Gomer Pyle USMC*.

Back to *Get Smart*, for which the premise was simple. Maxwell Smart was Agent 86, (the number was adapted from the expression "86 that," meaning "throw it out"), working for the organization CONTROL, which was based in Washington and charged with protecting the world from all enemies, particularly those supported by KAOS. These names were not

The Avengers and Get Smart

acronyms, by the way. Though fundamentally incompetent, Smart always triumphed, with assistance from his female partner, Agent 99 (her real name was never given), played by Barbara Feldon.

Born Barbara Hall, she was a former model who first gained public attention as a contestant on *The $64,000 Question*, specializing in Shakespeare, a subject she had studied in college. After three months' intense preparation, she indeed won $64,000. Feldon gained more notice in a commercial for "Top Brass," a men's hair cream. As she lay fetchingly on a tiger skin, she invited all of us "tigers out there" to avail ourselves of her product. When at the producer's suggestion Adams, who was about five-foot-seven, saw her in an episode of the television show *Mr. Broadway* starring Craig Stevens, he was taken aback at her height, but recognized that she was so right for the part that he dismissed the problem. Nonetheless, throughout the series Feldon almost always worked in flats or without shoes.

The third regular member of the team was the "Chief," played by Ed Platt. A trained opera singer and a powerful bass-baritone, his movie career included appearances with James Dean in *Rebel Without a Cause* and as Cary Grant's attorney in *North by Northwest*. In *Get Smart* he was the voice of authority, often frustrated by Max's gaffes, yet perpetually hopeful that Agent 86 would be able to carry out assignments. Platt provided what Buck Henry has called the "wall of reality" that buttressed the comedy (*Get Smart* Collection). Henry, we should note, served as story editor for the show's first two seasons, while once the pilot was accepted, Mel Brooks had little to do with the show.

Other semi-regular characters included Siegfried (Bernie Kopell), Smart's opposite number at KAOS, who bore a gaudy scar, spoke with an exaggerated Teutonic accent, and supervised his lumbering assistant played by King Moody and named Shtarker (a Yiddish word meaning a tough guy), as well as Agents 13 (Dave Ketchum) and 44 (Victor French), long-complaining colleagues stuck in absurd places like the inside of a clock or mailbox. Hymie the Robot (Dick Gautier) was created by a screwball scientist, but thanks to Max's influence worked on the side of CONTROL. He had superhuman powers, but obeyed commands literally, and thus the order to "hop to it, Hymie" sent him leaping about the room. During the first two seasons, Smart was also aided by Fang or Agent K-13, an endearing wolfhound.

What made the show appeal to its "erudite, well informed audience," as Executive Producer Stern described it? The first element was surely Adams' performance. He played Smart as a cocky bantam, with what Feldon has called "an innate swagger" (*Get Smart* Collection). He was also clumsy and oblivious to his own mistakes as well as much of what happened around him, but he was a vigorous fighter, both diligent and loyal.

The second element was the writing: crisp and unafraid to poke fun at the establishment. For instance, in one episode, after Max and 99 dispose of a KAOS assassin, she suffers a pang of conscience: "I wonder if we're any better." But Max reassures her: "We have to shoot and kill and destroy. We represent everything that's wholesome and good in the world."

Or when the Chief warns that an attack could "wipe out the city containing our finest minds and greatest leaders." Max is relieved: "Well, at least Washington is safe."

Some of the lines were predictable, yet still funny. Frequently the Chief announced some version of "Here's the plan," then delineated a scheme in great detail. As he spoke, Max nodded sagely, but once the Chief finished, the next sequence was inevitable:

> *Chief:* Have you got that?
>
> *Max:* Almost all of it, Chief.
>
> *Chief:* What didn't you get?
>
> *Max:* The part after "Here's the plan."

Henry has added that scripts were structured with physical humor for younger viewers and with verbal wit and satire for older ones *(Get Smart* Collection).

Third, I wonder if any television show has inspired as many catchphrases as *Get Smart*. One of the most famous was Max's familiar apology: "Sorry about that, Chief." Leonard Stern has commented that four weeks after the show premiered, he heard an astronaut in outer space invoke the phrase to one of his superiors (*Get Smart* Collection).

Equally addictive was "Would you believe . . . ?" which Dana and Adams originally wrote for Adams' standup act. In the show Max invoked it to bluff his way out of any number of seemingly impossible traps:

> *Max:* I happen to know that at this very moment, seven Coast Guard cutters are converging on this boat. Would you believe it? Seven.
>
> *Mr. Big:* I find that very difficult to believe.

Max:	How about six?
Mr. Big:	I don't thinks so.
Max:	How about two cops in a rowboat?

We cannot omit one more pattern. Frequently Max tried to plumb the depths of a crisis by saying, "Don't tell me that . . . ," then posing the worst possible contingency. The respondent immediately retorted with that very information, to which Max always answered: "I asked you not to tell me that."

Fourth, but vital, was the relationship between Max and 99, a pioneer in her own way: the first working woman in a sitcom. Moreover, her high number confirmed her status in CONTROL, and her skills and intelligence were never challenged. Feldon has stated that at the beginning of the series, her part was simply a job, and she never thought of herself as a feminist icon. During the run, however, and in the decades after, the number of girls and women who told her that she was an inspiration changed her mind. Indeed, Feldon has indicated that she and the character of 99 evolved together (*Get Smart* Collection). Her character never communicated hostility, nor was she ever manipulative. Instead she was always true to herself while maintaining devotion to Max (*Get Smart* Collection), whom she adored, but who viewed her as an agent first, then as a woman. Feldon is quoted as saying that what 99 saw in Max was the "willingness to go for it, against all odds, and recover. He had an indestructible zest and self-belief . . ." (Green 28). Creator Mel Brooks offered this perspective: "99 was a foil. She was George Burns, and 86 was actually Gracie Allen" (Green 41). Leonard Stern has written that "99 was the ultimate woman, someone everyone desires, who incorporated a sense of mischief with maternalism" (Green 41). In addition, Feldon has noted that Max's staccato delivery was an excellent contrast to her softer, more mellifluous voice. The subtleties of their relationship may be observed particularly well in the episode under consideration here: "Casablanca," written by Joseph C. Cavella and Carol Cavella, directed by William Wiard, and first broadcast October 22, 1966.

Parody was an essential aspect of *Get Smart*, which spoofed dozens of television shows and movies, including *Bonnie and Clyde*, *The Dirty Dozen*, *The Great Escape*, *The Maltese Falcon*, *Goldfinger*, *Ironside*, *Dr. No*, *Rear Window*, *Ship of Fools*, *The Fugitive*, and, here, the Bogart-Bergman classic *Casablanca*. Furthermore, within episodes the writers included innumerable cross-cultural references and multi-lingual puns, a lot for viewers to absorb. The series also featured appearances by dozens of guest stars. Some played substantial roles, like Adams's lifelong friend Don Rickles in "The Little Black Book," while most offered cameos, as when Johnny Carson appeared as a train conductor in "Aboard the Orient Express."

"Casablanca" begins in an airport terminal, where Smart is assigned to ensure that Dr. Pliny (the name belongs to an ancient Roman scholar) boards his plane safely. As the doctor prepares to buy flight insurance, Max stops him, noting that the Doctor has picked up a fountain pen, not a ballpoint. Claiming with characteristic Smart authority and with the unique Smart intonation that the fraudulent writing piece must have a detonator ("It takes a trained eye like mine to detect a thing like this"), Max insists that he will remove it. Max then opens the pen, and naturally the only substance that emerges is ink. Still, Max assures Dr. Pliny that danger as yet lurks: "The ink might activate the paper." Max's expression reveals that he knows he has blundered, but he still summons his dignity and calls the Chief. His device of transmission is a briefcase handle that turns into a phone, with the entire mechanism hidden in an airport locker.

Here is the moment to note that *Get Smart* employed hundreds of preposterous gadgets for communication, protection, and destruction. The most famous was Max's shoe phone, which he regularly removed and opened to dial calls. Once the series began, and for the rest of his life, Adams was perpetually greeted with shoes of all kinds, as patrons in restaurants or even passersby on the street would take off their own and shout some version of "It's the Chief!" The other device especially favored by Smart was the Cone of Silence, which Max insisted upon using whenever a conference in the Chief's office involved top-secret information. Unfortunately, once this double-headed plastic tube dropped over the speakers, they could never hear each other, while people outside discerned every word. Both inventions, by the way, were used in the pilot, a point of pride for co-writer Mel Brooks (Green 141). Meanwhile Smart's apartment was a hodgepodge of gizmos, ranging from nets that dropped from the ceiling, to desk ornaments that fired poisoned darts and bullets, to an invisible shield that fell and usually left Max on the wrong side.

These props became more and more outlandish, and were undoubtedly inspired by the extraordinary aids James Bond used in his filmed adventures. Eventually those contrivances, too, become so ludicrous that we can legitimately wonder whether the creators of the movies found inspiration in *Get Smart*.

The Avengers and *Get Smart*

At this moment in the show, Max calls the Chief to report that in exactly one minute and forty seconds, Dr. Pliny will be on his plane. The Chief, however, is unimpressed and orders Max to phone him back in one minute and forty-*one* seconds. As Max expresses dismay at the Chief's doubt, two gloved hands reach out from a locker and choke Pliny to death. When the Chief fears that Dr. Pliny is in trouble, Max looks over to find him dead on the floor, then warily replies: "That all depends . . . on whether his flight insurance covers being strangled in the terminal."

The trailer ends there, and what follows is one of the best title sequences for any series ever. As martial music plays and credits roll, Max drives in front of an office building, dashes inside, and marches down several flights of stairs, then through one set of iron doors after another. What makes the images so effective is Adams' persona. Dressed in black tie, he almost looks as if he knows what he's doing. At last he walks into a phone booth, drops in a coin, and dials; the floor beneath him opens, and he falls from sight.

Back in the airport, Max knocks on another locker and finds Agent 13 munching on a sandwich. "Didn't you hear or see anything at all?" Max asks, but Agent 13 explains that from twelve to one he has been on a lunch break. Max threatens his colleague with even more unpleasant stakeout positions, but 13 is unmoved. The image of two spies entrusted with the responsibility of countering threats against our nation and dickering this way is outlandish.

Back in the office, Max shows the Chief a tie as evidence, and the Chief concludes that the assassin must be "The Choker," who has killed 375 of the world's top scientists. The Chief calls The Choker "he," but Max postulates that the murderer could be a woman. Fortunately a witness has been found, a cab driver named Andrew Bubinski. ("Bubinski" is the Yiddish word for "bumbler"). This individual provides details about the look of the assassin, including "beady eyes," but unfortunately the subject he describes turns out to be Max.

The Chief has one clue where The Choker might be: the only plane leaving the airport at that time was headed for Casablanca. Max immediately volunteers to go, but the Chief fears that the Choker might recognize him. Besides, Max needs a "respite," and the Chief orders him on a two-week vacation. Now follows a delightful reversal of form. On many other episodes, the Chief regularly warned Max of the risks of a particular job, usually concluding with a phrase like ". . . and you'll be in mortal danger every minute." To which Max always replied, "And . . . *loving it.*" On this occasion Max threatens the Chief: "You'll be left all alone, without my experience and knowhow. You'll be making hundreds of decisions without my advice." To which The Chief counters: "And . . . *loving it.*"

In the lab, 99 models a disguise as an Eastern houseboy, but the Chief is convinced that no one will believe that 99 is male. Here is one of the few references in the series to how attractive Barbara Feldon was. After the Chief suggests an alternative costume, Max calls, asking to be reinstated on the case. In refusing the request, the Chief comments: "Your work is as good as it ever was." Max takes this reassurance as confirmation that he's back on the job, but the Chief denies the request: "Absolutely, positively, definitely, no!"

"Well, if you're undecided," replies Max, "I can call back."

When 99 returns, she is dressed in a slinky gown and adorned with a blond wig. Now the Chief is satisfied and informs her that she has been booked as a vocalist in the Bent Parrot Café in Casablanca. The name echoes "The Blue Parrot" from the original movie, and 99 recognizes the location: "The watering hole for the world's most notorious double agents." The Chief confirms her knowledge: "A melting pot for criminals of all races and creeds." Then 99 adds the topper: "And the headquarters of the Choker." That everyone knows exactly where spies gather suggests that the entire enterprise is ridiculous, one pervasive theme of the series.

The chief then explains that the café is noted for hiring "off-beat" singers. 99 modestly protests that she's not "off-beat" but "off-key," and we appreciate her sense of humor. She also cautions the Chief not to say anything about her taking over the case to Max, whose pride might be hurt, but the Chief assures her that Max is taking a two-week vacation in Canada. She's so relieved that she suggests that because the Chief looks tired, he could join Max: just the two of them alone in the cabin. As the Chief stares at her, her sentence trails off. No more need be said. Nonetheless, the moment shows the depth of her feelings for Max. She is his protector, who understands his weaknesses, but nonetheless supports him.

The scene shifts back to the airport where Max, dressed in heavy winter outerwear, enters escorted by the Chief. Once more Max asks permission to work on the case, but the Chief is resolute. Max is wounded: "You're supposed to be like a father to me." The Chief picks up the metaphor and tells Max to pretend he's going to camp. Now Max asks if he can home when he's homesick. "No," says the Chief, to which Max begins to whine: "Gee,

The Avengers and Get Smart

Dad—." But as soon as the Chief departs, Max's scoots from the Quebec plane to the one headed for Casablanca.

One more note. This series was shot long before our current airport security measures were instituted. Thus passengers could dash from one plane to another at the last minute. We can only imagine what fun the writers of *Get Smart* would have had with recent innovations.

The scene shifts to Casablanca, where 99 sings "They'll Be Some Changes Made." Her range is limited, as are her dancing skills, but she looks terrific, and the patrons, all of whom appear shifty, applaud generously. Meanwhile at the local airport, the passengers deplane, sweating profusely. Then Max staggers in, still for some reason wearing his wool cap, thick gloves, and winter coat. An airport official asks if he is an American tourist. "Tremendous guess," says Max. The official explains that the temperature is 101 degrees, but Max refuses to admit his error in apparel: "Well, I happen to find it quite cool," and pats his arms once before beginning a familiar routine.

"I find that very hard to believe," says the airport attendant.

"Would you believe . . . comfortably cool?" replies Max.

"I don't think so."

"How do the words 'heat prostration' grab you?"

Back at the Bent Parrot, 99 sings again, this time the French classic "La Vie En Rose." In the middle of her song, Max enters, now suitably dressed and with a cigarette trailing from his mouth in the unmistakable style of Humphrey Bogart. As he sits at the bar and watches 99, she notices him, and the two measure each other. Meanwhile Max performs all of Bogart's familiar mannerisms: the squinting of the eyes, the stroking of the chin, and the pulling of the ear. He tries a drink, but forgets to remove the cigarette, which becomes sodden with liquor. Nonetheless, with dignity intact, he resumes puffing.

Backstage at the bar, Max calls CONTROL. The operator requests money for the first three payments, but Max explains that he's calling from his shoe. "Is that a private shoe?" the operator asks. Eventually the connection is made, and Max inquires about 99. The Chief pretends that she's in the next room, but Max is more concerned that the choker may be a woman. The Chief advises him to forget about the case and to "Try not to get frostbite."

"That I can promise you," says Max.

Immediately 99 calls the Chief to explain that a man in the bar looks exactly like Max. Could that cab driver have been right? After the Chief weighs the possibility, the two agree to put Plan 7 into effect (whatever that is). The Chief, however, warns 99: "You're dealing with a deadly assassin. Don't let the fact that he looks like Max slow your reflexes. If he makes one questionable move . . ." 99 wistfully finishes the thought: "I'll know it's not Max." We don't want to make too much out of a single line in such a frothy concoction, but this sentence reflects all the frustration and longing that characterized 99.

Next Max strolls into the bar, smoking wearily. He sits at a table, where a waiter brings him a drink. Immediately a massive figure that we see only from the back joins him, and begins speaking in a voice reminiscent of Sidney Greenstreet, a figure familiar from the original movie. This man mutters something about expecting Max, who first uses his own voice, then switches to a fine Bogart impression. The intruder explains that "they" are about to overthrow "the government," but Smart challenges him: "Not so fast, fat man. Which government?" The answer is obvious: "What does it matter, as long as we make a profit?" The "fat man" then offers one of Greenstreet's archetypal giggles and departs. His place is taken by a smaller figure, speaking in the sinister nasal whisper of Peter Lorre: "Did you get the information?" Now Max is in full Bogart mode: "Look, buster, Do you know what's gonna happen if Sophia sees me talkin' to you? He's gonna slap my teeth out, then kick me in the stomach for mumbling. Get lost." The faux noir dialogue is nonsensical but appropriate.

As Max lights another cigarette, he is joined by 99, who challenges him to give her one: "Ladies first." Smart maintains the patter: "Ladies ask." To which 99 replies" Light me." Both actors are clearly enjoying themselves. As 99 kisses Max's hand, he makes a counteroffer: "Why don't you let me order you a ham sandwich?" She then invites him to her dressing room, but Max has trepidations: "What am I going to get in your dressing room that I can't get here?" "Me" is the classic noir reply.

On the way backstage, Max turns to the pianist and utters the most celebrated, if misquoted, line from the original movie: "Play it again, Sam." The pianist retorts "My name ain't Sam," but Max is unflappable: "Don't confuse me. I'm new in Casablanca."

In 99's dressing room, as Max searches her possessions, the man we recognize as The Choker trails him, but then 99 enters and demands to know Max's purpose. He maintains character: "Well, I could say I'm

The Avengers and Get Smart

looking for the Maltese Falcon, but you'd never believe me." 99, however, is undeterred, and the two begin a cross-examination:

"Are you or are you not Max?'

"Max who?"

"Maxwell Smart."

"I might ask you the same question."

"Ask it."

"Are you or are you not Maxwell Smart?"

"If you are Maxwell Smart, you better speak up fast before it's too late."

"I'm no more Maxwell Smart than you are 99."

Despite the silliness of the situation, amusing tension is created.

Finally the two recognize each other and admit that both thought the other was somewhere else. 99 is especially relieved, and before they exchange information, goes to change clothes. Max is convinced that The Choker is "5000 miles from here," but 99 believes he could be "closer than we think." As she speaks, The Choker comes from behind the curtain and seems to strangle Max, then go after 99, but Max suddenly stands and shoots him. 99 is astounded that Max is all right, but he has an explanation: "He fell for the old false neck trick."

Here's another of the verbal patterns that recurred throughout the series. Max was forever bemoaning how opponents conjured strategies that fooled him: "The old gas-mask-in-the-false-nose trick" or "The old airplane-in-the-haystack trick" or even "The old Professor-Peter-Peckinpaugh-all-purpose-anti-personnel-Peckinpaugh-pocket-pistol-under-the-toupee trick." Sometimes in his frustration Max added: "That's the second time I fell for it this month."

In this scene we also note that 99 does not physically defend herself against attack from the Choker. Feldon has indicated that at the start of the series, the writers asked her to perform karate chops and other such maneuvers, but as hard as she tried, she was unconvincing. This vulnerability was a sharp contrast with the character that Feldon has confessed was in some ways her role model, Diana Rigg as Emma Peel, who could be tough and unsmiling. But, of course, as Feldon has noted, the two women had vastly different partners, and to sustain Max 99 had to be more accommodating.

In the tag, the three main characters reconnoiter in the Chief's office. Here 99 is dressed in her own clothes, which were always modern and stunning, another way she was a forerunner. Throughout the series her wardrobe contrasted dramatically with the formal wear of the late 50s and early 60s, and her manner of dress lent an aura of independence that complemented her job and attitude. Like Emma Peel's outfits, 99's both set her apart and communicated her humor and spirit of adventure. Here, after the Chief congratulates her for a "particularly fine job," 99 acknowledges that she "enjoyed every minute" and that perhaps "blondes do have more fun," echoing the famous commercial of that time. But in fact Feldon was more attractive as a brunette.

The Chief admires Max's "false neck," and asks where he acquired such an "ingenious device." Max's answer is predictable: "The ingenious device department." Impressed, the Chief next asks how Max recognized 99, giving Max a chance to run on professionally about her walk and her vocal characteristics. He admits, though, that what convinced him was the way she said two words: "I'm 99." As usual 99 punctures Max's image just a bit by asking how Max would have identified her if she hadn't spoken, but Max insists that with his unerring sense of smell he would have recognized her cologne: "seductive, soft, feminine, mysterious." For a moment we think Max might be aroused, but 99 clarifies that she is not wearing any perfume. At this confession, both turn to the Chief, who self-consciously coughs and resumes shuffling papers.

So many other shows from this series offered similar pleasures. I've always been partial to those that feature Harry Hoo, a Chinese detective with whom Max trades aphorisms and deductions. Except that none of Max's pronouncements make any sense, inspiring Hoo regularly to respond "A-maz-ing!" more in disbelief than admiration. "The Man from Yenta" brings Israeli agent 498 (marked down from 500), who is charged to protect visiting Prince Ali Ben Bubee. When 498 arrives at the airport, Smart immediately begins to outline their plans, but 498 protests: "Wait a minute! Aren't you going to ask how was my flight?" Smart obliges: "How was your flight?" Even as a first-time viewer, I said the next line in sync with 498: "Don't ask." And in "The King Lives?" Max plays a dual role as the King of Caronia, a role that offered Adams another opportunity to demonstrate his versatility by imitating Ronald Colman.

After the third season of *Great Smart*, ratings began to slip, so the writers arranged for Max and 99 to marry. During the fifth season, the couple actually had twins, and most of the stories were complicated by 99's pregnancy. Though these plot developments temporarily saved *Get Smart*, here was when the series "jumped the shark." That phrase is taken from an episode of *Happy Days* when Fonzie, waterskiing while wearing a leather jacket, literally "jumps" a shark. But the idiom is now applied when the quality of any show has declined so far that writers and producers invent gimmicks that usually fail to salvage the program, precisely the fate of *Get Smart*. Part of the fun of the original episodes was the lack of romance, as Max was too self-involved to appreciate 99's amorous feelings. Once romance began to blossom, however, real-life problems intruded, and in truth Max had no place in the real world. Even worse, 99's giving birth to twins gave rise to the terrifying possibility that chronically clumsy Max would be responsible for the well-being of two infants. From the start of the series Mel Brooks and Buck Henry fought to ensure that it would not be laden with domesticity, and after Brooks's departure, Henry as story editor maintained that approach. Thus the inclusion of romance not only became the beginning of the end, but also justified Brooks's and Henry's vision.

The initial run of *Get Smart* ended in March of 1969. Adams and Feldon reprised their characters in the 1980 movie *The Nude Bomb*, then briefly in a 1995 series, but neither enterprise succeeded. The Smart franchise was brought back in a 2008 version starring Steve Carell and Anne Hathaway, which proved more popular.

After the series ended Adams tried various shows, but he was essentially typecast, although he did find success in voiceovers, particularly as Inspector Gadget. He died in 2005.

Barbara Feldon played a variety of parts on television and in movies, but some time ago explained that although she would always be proud of her work on *Get Smart*, she had no more interest in performing. Divorced since 1967, she lives in New York City and has published a book, *Living Alone and Loving It*.

As noted, Edward Platt died in 1975.

To probe for deeper meaning to *Get Smart* may seem foolish. Certainly the series' prime purpose was to create fun, pure and simple, but underneath the laughter a few themes did shine through. One was the eternal hope that good will ultimately triumph, because, after all, Max did win out. Second, we saw the absurd extremes to which both sides, CONTROL and KAOS, resorted. Finally, the show implied that we should be skeptical of all official institutions, especially those that hide from public scrutiny. The more secretive they are, and the more they insist on their need for such confidentiality, the more dangerous they usually are. The same lessons may be inferred from *The Avengers*.

Finally, let me close with a word about Mrs. Peel and 99, both of whom found a permanent place in my heart. When in my imagination I was smooth, tough, and witty, I envisioned spending time in the fast-paced and dangerous company of Mrs. Peel. When I saw myself as less dynamic but nonetheless noble and nurturing, as well as a touch frisky, I fancied devoting my energies to making 99 happy.

Together they brought out my best.

VI

The Honeymooners
"The Golfer"

and

All in the Family
"Judging Books By Their Covers"

In the fall of 1976 I joined the faculty of Pomfret School, located in the northeastern Connecticut town of the same name. Among my responsibilities was sophomore English, and among the works I assigned was a play I had read in high school, but never taught: Arthur Miller's *Death of a Salesman*.

During our first session with the script, students offered reactions to it, and many of these focused on the relationship between Willy Loman ("the Salesman") and his sons, Biff and Happy. Several students referred to their own family, particularly fathers or grandfathers to whom Willy seemed similar. After the pace of response slowed, I posed a question of my own: "Does Willy Loman remind you of any other characters from drama?" No one replied, so I framed my question more directly: "I'm thinking particularly of television." At once hands went up, and two names were cited: Ralph Kramden of *The Honeymooners* and Archie Bunker of *All in the Family*, then in the middle of its first run.

WALKING DISTANCE

One detour. By the year 2000, when I had been teaching in college for nearly twenty years, some of my students still remembered hearing or reading about these programs; only a few, however, had actually seen them. By 2010, not a single student remembered either the shows or any of the characters or actors.

Back in 1976, though, Ralph and Archie were familiar to virtually every member of my class, and we devoted time to exploring what they had in common with the already iconic protagonist of *Death of a Salesman*.

All three characters lived in the outer boroughs of New York City: Willy and Ralph in Brooklyn, Archie in Queens.

All were cognizant of their age. Willy was in his early sixties, Archie was in his fifties, and Ralph was about forty.

All felt burdened by demanding blue-collar jobs. Willy, of course, was a salesman, driving for weeks at a time through New England, hauling sample cases in and out of his car. Archie worked on a loading dock. Ralph (do I even have to mention this?) was a bus driver who returned home exhausted virtually every night.

All worried about money.

All had wives who worked only at home and kept the family intact. All these women were smarter, or at least more thoughtful, than their husbands.

All three men often felt trapped in their lives

All had tempers, and all regularly became angry.

All sometimes took out their anger on their wives.

Willy did share salient characteristics with only one of the other two. For instance, Willy and Ralph lived in the decade following the end of World War II, while Archie's time frame was the primarily the 1970s.

Willy also spent his life seeking schemes that would make money. When he was younger, he considered joining his brother, Ben, in Alaska, and in Willy's memory Ben continually exults over his own success: ". . . when I walked into the jungle I was seventeen. When I walked out, I was twenty-one. And, by God, I was rich!" (Miller 52). Now when Willy's sons propose forming two water polo teams or boxing each other to sell sporting goods, Willy seizes the idea: "Lick the civilized world! You guys together could absolutely lick the civilized world (Miller 64).

Ralph Kramden also regularly conjured up schemes for making money. Some were piddling, as when he fashioned a homemade Halloween costume to win the $50 first prize at his lodge. Some were more elaborate,

The Honeymooners and *All in the Family*

as when he bought thousands of Handy Housewife Helpers and tried to sell them for profit via a live commercial on television.

Willy and Archie, too, shared an important value: both deeply believed in what they judged to be strong American values.

In speaking to his sons, for instance, Willy glorifies his country: "America is full of beautiful towns and fine upstanding people" (Miller 31). He often talks about his sons' possibilities for success, his version of what we know as "the American Dream."

Archie fought in World War II and still considered himself a patriot of the first order. In seemingly every episode, he extolled the greatness of America. Or at least how he imagined the country *used to be.*

Here's where one of my students noted a crucial difference between Bunker and the other two characters. Archie constantly fulminated against African Americans, Jews, Puerto Ricans, Italians, Irishmen, Asians, Poles (especially his son-in-law), and any other ethnic group that might be mentioned. He also couched his resentment in harsh terms, invoking ugly epithets and stereotypes. True, his beliefs were dramatized as misguided, and Archie himself was regularly proven wrong, but even in the face of overwhelming evidence he maintained his prejudices.

Members of my class immediately agreed that this trait of Archie's differentiated him from the other two characters, so to provoke more discussion, I turned to a passage from the first act of *Death of a Salesman,* when Willy articulates some of his anger: "There's more people! That's what's ruining this country! Population is getting out of control! The competition is maddening! Smell the stink from that apartment house! And another one on the other side . . ." (Miller 17–18). I then suggested that we could easily imagine Willy's outburst against people in general turning into one of Archie's diatribes against a specific group. The common thread, I suggested, was that neither man accepted the changes occurring in the country that both prized.

While we pondered this assertion, the students and I recalled favorite moments from the two television series. Eventually we came to a conclusion, one that still seems to me true: although the programs were ostensibly comedies, underneath the laughter lurked profound unhappiness. The shows were not tragedies like *Death of a Salesman,* but however much we enjoyed the comic situations and the characters' foibles, *The Honeymooners* often skirted the edge of tragedy, while *All in the Family* sometimes faced tragedy head-on.

Here is the heart of how these two shows differed most significantly from the other comedy series discussed in this book. *The Phil Silvers Show* and *McHale's Navy* occasionally hinted at genuine feelings, but never for long and never to lasting effect. In *The Dick Van Dyke Show* and *The Andy Griffith Show,* characters sometimes endured unhappiness, but it almost always resolved comfortably. In *The Honeymooners,* on the other hand, people genuinely suffered, and at the end of certain episodes, their pain lingered. Finally in *All in the Family,* the anguish that characters experienced sometimes remained unabated, and viewers were forced to accept that life doesn't always have a happy ending.

Let's begin with *The Honeymooners* and its star, the primal force known as Jackie Gleason. Born in 1916 in the Bushwick section of Brooklyn, he endured a painful, poverty-stricken childhood. His older brother died when Jackie was three, his father soon deserted the family, and his mother died a few years later. For a time Jackie spent his days shooting pool and running with gangs, but eventually caught the show business bug, and with a friend put together an act. They were booked into small clubs throughout the Northeast, engagements that led him back to New York City, then over the next decade to an undistinguished career in clubs and movies. He received his biggest break in the fledging business of television, starring in 1949 in the title role in *The Life of Riley,* but the show was cancelled after only one year (although it returned in 1953 for a five-year run starring William Bendix). Gleason's performance, however, in combination with attention gained through his work in California nightclubs, led to his next opportunity: as one of the rotating hosts of the Dumont network's *Cavalcade of Stars.* He soon understood that the small screen was his ideal medium, and with his limitless self-confidence and skill at physical comedy, an unlikely attribute considering his girth, American audiences embraced him. His weekly demand to the orchestra leader for "a little traveling music" to accompany him into the wings, followed by his signature "And away we go!" became national catch phrases. Here is also where he cultivated his one-man repertory company, including Reginald Van Gleason III, a millionaire complete with top hat and cape and a penchant for drink; the befuddled and silent Poor Soul; Joe the Bartender; and Ralph Kramden, who initially was part of a recurring sketch featuring a bickering couple ironically called "The Honeymooners." When the show moved to CBS and was retitled *The Jackie Gleason Show,* the characters moved with it, and in 1955 *The Honeymooners* became a regular half-hour series. Although its ratings were strong, Gleason ended production in 1956, leaving behind just one season of episodes, now known as "The Classic Thirty-Nine." The shows were filmed with a new higher-quality process called "Electronicam," an investment by Gleason that proved wise, for the complete series has since been replayed innumerable times around this country and the world.

Those original sketches on the *Cavalcade* were considerably harsher than the episodes of the later series. The set was bare and gloomy, a recreation of Gleason's boyhood home at 328 Chauncey Street. Ralph Kramden was a miserable, bitter man, married to an equally unhappy older woman, played by Pert Kelton, and the couple lived perpetually burdened by financial problems. Ed and Trixie Norton, who resided upstairs, were added later. Ed (Art Carney) was a sewer worker, a job that might have given rise to resentment from him. Yet he romanticized his work, and generally appeared much happier than Ralph. Trixie (originally played by Elaine Stritch) was a former burlesque dancer, but Stritch was replaced after one show by Joyce Randolph, a less glamorous and much less abrasive figure. When *The Honeymooners* became a regular series, Kelton, too, was replaced, ostensibly because of a heart condition, but in fact because she had been blacklisted over her husband's political connections. Gleason was initially wary of casting Audrey Meadows as Alice, fearing she was too attractive, but when he saw her dressed plainly and without makeup, he was convinced.

That one season was filmed under extraordinary circumstances. Gleason was the absolute authority on every aspect of production, including the theme song he wrote, but he loathed rehearsing, which he believed throttled spontaneity and therefore believability. He himself possessed a photographic memory, so after reading a script once or twice, he felt confident to take the stage. The other actors, however, were accustomed to more preparation, and thus were compelled to run through scenes with Jackie's stand-in. Gleason also liked to ad-lib, but was understandably prone to forget lines; therefore his fellow cast members, as well as the small roster of regular supporting players, performed on the edge, and learned to rely on one another. Each program was filmed before a live audience, and virtually all mistakes were incorporated into the show. No doubt the tension during filming is one reason the shows still possess such energy and realistic feeling.

In the series the Kramden apartment remained starkly furnished: a kitchen table with cloth and chairs, a stove, a small ancient icebox, a sink, a dresser, and an offstage bedroom. The couple had no phone (although one was installed during a later episode) and no television (although early in the series they temporarily acquired one). Oddly, even though Ralph and Ed made the same $62 a week, our few glimpses of the Nortons' apartment suggested that this couple enjoyed more comforts, but only because Norton was willing to accept debt, while Ralph prided himself on his thrift. Occasionally the scripts required other settings, but all were simple. Both couples were also childless, another Gleason edict, for he believed a youngster would be unable to maintain the chaotic rehearsal schedule Gleason required.

Of the "Classic Thirty-Nine," none is more beloved than "The Golfer," written by A. J. Russell and Herbert Finn, directed (in name only) by Frank Satenstein, and originally broadcast on October 15, 1955. The opening scene is set in a room at the bus company that serves as a cafeteria as well as a locker area. A driver (played by Gleason regular George Petrie) rushes in to report that Ralph Kramden is likely to be the new assistant traffic manager. One listener is skeptical, as are a couple of other personnel. But when Ralph enters, he does so with his familiar bravado, as well as cigars for everyone. Viewers who have seen even a couple of shows from the series recognize the situation. Even as Ralph cautions that the offer is not yet firm, he cannot resist boasting. He also requests that the other men not tell Norton, who will be joining Ralph for lunch: "You know what a big blabbermouth he is." And Ralph wants the pleasure of telling Alice himself.

Whenever I see this scene, I'm reminded of a line near the end of *Death of a Salesman*, when Charley, Willy's neighbor, explains that Bernard, Charley's son and Biff's boyhood friend, will argue a case in front of the Supreme Court. Willy marvels: "And he didn't even mention it!" To which Charley answers: "He don't have to—he's gonna do it" (Miller 95). That lesson is one that Ralph Kramden never learns.

Norton soon arrives, and Ralph immediately blurts out the news. Norton is overjoyed, but then Ralph's buddies start to track down the source of the rumor, which naturally turns out to be Ralph himself. At that moment, Gleason's transformation is remarkable. From an overbearing braggart, he turns almost instantly into a helpless child, caught in a lie and desperate not to be punished. This brief scene reminds us what a superb actor Gleason was.

One of the other drivers claims that their boss, Mr. Harper, doesn't even know that Ralph is alive. When the others leave, Ralph in a characteristic outburst insists that he has worked hard and deserves the promotion.

The Honeymooners and All in the Family

Unfortunately he just doesn't have the connections, and without those even the smartest guy in the world can't get ahead. Here's another echo from *Death of a Salesman*. As Willy says: ". . . it's not what you do. Ben. It's who you know and the smile on your face" (Miller 86). In this episode, however, Norton comically disagrees: "I didn't have no connections when I got my job in the sewer."

A few words are appropriate here about the man playing Norton, Art Carney. Gleason often said that 90% of the success of *The Honeymooners* belonged to Carney, and although the star was surely exaggerating, Carney was indeed indispensable. In the 30s and 40s he had enjoyed a career in radio, singing and doing various voices. In 1950, when Gleason's *Cavalcade of Stars* needed an actor to play the mild-mannered counterpart of Gleason's loudmouth, Charlie Bratton, Carney was hired, and the two performers established an extraordinary rapport. Carney's later career included a Best Actor Academy Award in 1974 for *Harry and Tonto*, and on Broadway he was the original Felix Unger in Neil Simon's *The Odd Couple*, opposite first Walter Matthau and later Jack Klugman as Oscar Madison. The role of Ed Norton, however, brought his greatest fame.

Norton (as everyone called him, including Ralph and Trixie) was good-natured and optimistic, everything Ralph Kramden was not. He wasn't any smarter than Ralph, but he lacked Ralph's desperation to climb. The reason may be that Norton had the capacity to find pleasure in the simplest things. Whereas Ralph continually struggled toward imagined wealth, Norton could savor a slice of pizza, stickball with some street kids, or a game of pool. But perhaps Norton's most important contribution was that no matter how much abuse Ralph hurled at him, Norton always forgave. He intuited that beneath Ralph's hectoring was a well-meaning, if understandably angry, man. In one episode, for instance, Ralph and Norton each list the other's good qualities. Ralph ponders the matter and proceeds slowly, but Norton finishes in seconds. When Ralph characteristically explodes over why Norton can't think of anything else to write, Norton calmly reveals his list: "Ralph Kramden is the sweetest kid in the world." That Norton nurtured such affection, despite all of Ralph's mistreatment, permitted viewers to feel the same way.

One other point that we'll develop presently. Vocally and physically, Carney was, to borrow one of Ralph's favorite words, "a riot."

Here Norton invites Ralph to eat outside, but Ralph has another idea: he will wait for Mr. Harper and engage him in conversation. Norton suggests that Ralph should explain how he hasn't any connections, but Ralph proposes another strategy: he will casually banter about Mr. Harper himself. Norton approves, then pulls out a gigantic hero sandwich and invites Ralph to "start at the other end." Ralph declines, but before Norton actually bites this monstrosity, he indulges in some of his unique stage business, flattening and measuring it until Ralph, who has watched in wonder, shouts: "Will you stop that!" Norton carries out a similar routine under various circumstances and with various props, but most famously in preparing to sign his name, when he turns that simple act into an elaborate ritual of loosening his wrists and shoulders that drives Ralph to distraction: "*Will you come on*!?"

At this point Mr. Harper conveniently appears, and Ralph sidles up to him. First Ralph inquires about Mr. Harper's children, but Mr. Harper grumpily replies that he has none. Ralph then mentions Mr. Harper's wife, but Mr. Harper responds that he is not married. Finally Ralph asks about Mr. Harper himself, then laughs with phony heartiness: "Got you that time!" Mr. Harper, though, remains unimpressed.

When Harper picks up his golf clubs, Ralph seizes the opportunity to make conversation. He resists claiming to play himself, but Norton leaps up to laud Ralph's abilities: "You put a club in this lad's hands, and he's dynamite!" Mr. Harper seems eager to have Ralph join him, but can't set a time. Norton, however, is relentless, and despite Ralph's arm-waving, the match is arranged: four weeks from Saturday. Ralph's helplessness is revealed through his familiar stumbling response to the invitation: "Homina, homina, homina, homina." As Mr. Harper leaves, hinting that he'll see Ralph soon, Ralph pretends to be pleased, but when the door closes, he confesses his ignorance about golf and berates Norton for getting Ralph involved: "I don't even know where left field is!" Norton, however, has a solution: by the time Ralph is supposed to play, he'll already have the job, and be able to back out. And if by chance he does have to play, Norton will be there to help. At this claim Ralph is taken aback: how can Norton possibly help him? Simple, replies Norton. Golf has eighteen holes, and after ten years in the sewer, he's certainly an expert on holes.

The scene reveals the heart of these two characters. In front of Norton, Ralph overflows with bombast, but when faced with real authority shrivels to helplessness. Norton initially seems confused, but when he grasps an idea he becomes carried away. Like Laurel and Hardy, to whom Ralph and Ed have frequently been compared, both men were essentially boys,

The Honeymooners and All in the Family

another reason a child would not fit in either household. And like boys, Ralph and Ed required an adult to extricate them from the dilemmas in which they unthinkingly placed themselves.

That adult appears in the next scene, set in the Kramden apartment, where Alice is in the bedroom and Ralph calls to tell her his news. When Alice ignores this bulletin and instead requests that he take out the garbage, an exasperated Ralph asserts that he won't need his lunchbox any more: "Oh, Ralph, you're going on a diet!" Alice says. Ralph insists that he's not, so she assumes the opposite: "Are you getting a bigger lunchbox?" Now Ralph is peeved, and because of that "snide remark" threatens never to tell her. Alice, however, doesn't mind, and leaves Ralph to stew. Eventually he cannot withhold word about the job, but is forced to confess that it's not official yet. All Alice says, is "Oh," but she thereby sets off another Kramden tirade about how she heartlessly assumes that his dreams will never come true. All the while Ralph (or should I say "Gleason") paces behind the kitchen table, sometimes pushing Meadows out of the way. The more we see of *The Honeymooners*, the more we realize how limited the direction is. The other actors tend to move only a little, but Gleason strides around the small playing area, waving his arms as he bellows. Yet he does not steal focus. His attention is fixed on the other actors, who stand still and listen. We in turn watch them watching him.

When Ralph finally discloses his scheme that he expects will land him the job before he must play golf, Alice expresses her usual doubts, but Ralph assures her that she, too, will benefit. No longer will she have to rush to 42nd Street and Madison Avenue in Manhattan to deliver a message to him. Instead the Kramdens will have a phone so she can reach "the assistant traffic manager." Alice, however, already knows what she'll call to tell him: "When are you going to take the garbage out"?

The argument is interrupted by one of Ralph's bus driver buddies from the previous scene, the same George Petrie, here called "Freddy," and who appeared in a couple of dozen episodes in multiple guises. He claims to have good news from Mr. Harper, and at once Ralph preens about how close he and Harper have become. Indeed, even Freddy is convinced that if Ralph can do this one favor, the assistant traffic manager's job will be his.

What's the favor? To play golf on Sunday.

As Ralph stares blankly, Freddy grabs his hand: "It certainly looks like you're going places." After Freddy leaves, though, Alice just nods; "As long as you're going places . . . would you mind taking the garbage?" This line, delivered with complete deadpan by Meadows, leads to the commercial break.

Alice's capacity for repartee was one of the vital elements of the series. No matter how much Ralph yelled, she was never intimidated. Indeed, whenever he went too far, as happened in almost every episode, she was the one who brought him back to reality. Had she not been as strong as she was, Ralph would have come off as a bully mistreating an abused wife, but because of Alice's resilience, we knew that Ralph would be put in his place.

The scene after the break is perhaps the most celebrated in the series. Ralph enters, dressed in a grotesque parody of a golfing outfit. Even in black and white, we feel the absurd clash of plaid and argyle. As recorded in *The Official Honeymooners Treasury*, the other cast members rehearsed in costume, but Gleason donned his outfits only for the actual shooting. Thus this particular appearance left everyone laughing (Crescenti and Columbe 21).

Ralph enters swinging wildly, but part of what makes his clumsiness enjoyable is our knowledge that Gleason was a superb golfer. To look as bad as he does in the following moments takes real skill. He then shouts out the window for Norton, who almost immediately appears downstairs, inspiring a shout of distress from Ralph. We also note that Norton fails to close the outside door.

Norton admires Ralph's outfit: "Deevine!" But although Ralph appreciates the generous comment, his first priority is a golf ball. In response, Norton removes from his pocket something that he explains is a pin cushion. What follows next is probably one of the many miscues that fans of the show are delighted to cite. Norton puts the pin cushion on the floor, but Ralph corrects him: "C'mon, pal, let me have it." In life Gleason called most people "pal," and here he momentarily breaks character, as Carney seems to have forgotten the bit. Ed then hands Ralph the pin cushion, but Ralph yelps in pain, shocked to find real pins. Norton, though, has an explanation: "What do you expect in a pin cushion? Chicken noodles?" Norton then removes the pins, but with a singular twist: "She loves me, she loves me not—" until Ralph slaps his shoulder: "Will you cut that out?" Every one of Norton's moves here is a gem.

Norton offers to read instructions from a book, but Ralph claims not to have time to listen. Instead he swings twice, misses, then blames the club. By the way, each swing is exactly the same and actually starts back correctly. What Gleason does wrong is the downswing, as his club always strikes the floor a foot behind the ball. The precision is impressive. Sensing a need

The Honeymooners and *All in the Family*

for help, Ralph reluctantly asks Norton to read, and Ed obliges: "To Emily, whose slice inspired me to write this book." Ralph naturally explodes.

What follows is the most famous single moment from the entire series. First Ed reads the initial lesson: "Step up, plant your feet firmly, and address the ball." The last directive puzzles Ralph, but Norton has a solution. He steps up, plants his feet firmly, and salutes the pin cushion: "Helloooooo, ball!" The laughter and applause are overwhelming.

In and of itself, the line is funny. What makes it triumphant is the extraordinary delivery.

I cannot count how often I have played golf with strangers, especially older gentlemen, and watched one player step up to the tee, put down his ball, plant his feet, and offer his version of "Helloooooo, ball!" The line is universally recognized. Fittingly enough, the moment was created entirely by Art Carney, to whom Gleason was always pleased to assign the best comic bits.

After recovering from Norton's performance, Ralph asks him to read further. What follows is a series of instructions familiar to anyone who has ever taken a golf lesson: left arm straight, head down, knees bent, and eyes on the ball, among others. But when Ralph swings, he manages to wrap the club against his neck. As he cries in agony, he begins to doubt that he can learn golf in two days: "It'll take at least a week." Norton, however, refuses to be discouraged, and offers his own version of the swing. He once again "addresses" the ball, rotates his waist in a circle, loosens his knees by making them oscillate with astonishing speed, and finally swings. Only his hat goes flying.

Carney's gestures and balance are remarkable. I always wonder how much of it was prepared, and how much was ad libbed. Much of the latter, I suspect.

Ralph stares in amazement, then inquires ironically whether he is supposed to perform those same gyrations. As the audience howls, he even imitates them. To relieve his pal's anguish, Norton proposes swinging without the ball, a prospect which Ralph approves. Thus he imitates Norton's moves as closely as possible, rotating his own massive waist, then swinging. The result pleases him, so Norton suggests that they move to problem shots, like hitting on a hill. Norton keeps raising the obstacle until Ralph explodes once more: "Who am I playing with? Mr. Harper or a mountain goat?"

As Ralph prepares his shot, the door opens wide, and Alice enters directly in the middle of his backswing. Ralph immediately becomes sheepish: "Just practicing golf." Alice returns a characteristically withering retort: "Is that what it is? I thought it was football, the way your backfield was in motion." Here's just one of the countless lines the writers invented to comment on Ralph's weight.

Alice tries to inject common sense, but Ralph insists that he's hitting shots all over the place: "You can't discourage me. I have enough confidence in me for the both of us." Gleason articulates this line boastfully, setting up Alice's classic response: "You have enough *everything* in you for the both of us." Alice then retreats to the bedroom, but not before Ralph hurls one of his classic sallies: "How'd you like to go sailing over the clubhouse?"

This idle line is a modest version of a *Honeymooners'* staple: Ralph's regular threats of violence against Alice. Sometimes he said, "One of these days, Alice. One of these days. Pow! Right in the kisser!" Other times he phrased himself more colorfully: "How'd you like to go to the moon?" Or with a cartoon-like "Bang! Zoom" emphasized with appropriate gestures. No doubt Gleason heard some of these phrases at home when he was a boy, and in the 1950s they were viewed as little more than comic badgering, because viewers knew that Ralph would never, *could never*, harm Alice. These days, though, the lines resonate differently. We are more sensitive to the problem of domestic violence, and Ralph's behavior comes uncomfortably close. Nevertheless, what makes these outbursts tolerable is, first, Alice's resolve. Whatever Ralph says, she looks directly at him, and her sharp tone squelches him. Second, as soon as she does give him one of those looks, Ralph backs down. He knows when he has crossed a line, and he shamefacedly retreats. Third, and perhaps most important, we know that Ralph is devoted to Alice. The passionate kiss at the end of almost every episode, preceded by Ralph's declaration "Baby, you're the greatest," was affirmation of what we sensed all along. Thus just as Alice forgave Ralph's blunders and braggadocio, so did we.

Back in the "The Golfer," Norton tries to settle Ralph's nerves for one more practice swing. Ed puts the pin cushion on the floor (much closer to the wall, we notice), then runs down that list of instructions. Ralph follows each directive, then swings and smashes the club into a pile of pots, simultaneously breaking its head. Now even he sees the futility of his efforts.

The final scene takes place in the kitchen, with Ralph sitting at the table in a panic: "What am I gonna do?" Alice can only ask, "Ralph, why do you get yourself into spots like this?" Ralph's explanation is simple: "Because I have a BIG MOUTH!" And as he says those two words his mouth opens appropriately wide. Still, he offers reassurance: "But I learned my lesson this time." This claim is followed by a knock at the door, which Ralph answers to find one of the Vice-Presidents of the bus company, Mr. Douglas, who reports that Mr. Harper chipped a bone in his ankle and won't be able to play for months. In response, Ralph alternates between feigned disappointment and legitimate joy, but within seconds cannot help reverting to his normal self and his imaginary golfing skills: "I don't like to brag . . ." He even claims that he intended to give Mr. Harper "some pointers, some tricks," and snaps his fingers with pride. Meanwhile behind him, Alice's face darkens. Mr. Douglas, however, has a solution: he will take Mr. Harper's place on the golf course. This news naturally leaves Ralph speechless, so after Douglas closes the door behind him, Ralph assesses the situation: "Well, Alice, you gotta admit one thing: I gotta BIG MOUTH!"

This dénouement does not involve the usual kiss and expression of love and forgiveness, but those generally followed when Ralph had wronged Alice herself. Here he has made just himself look foolish. But the final minutes of this story remind us that people don't really change, and at this moment Ralph is what he will always be.

To mention any more episodes from "The Classic Thirty-Nine" is unnecessary. Each is a gem. Many years after the series ended, Gleason was asked why *The Honeymooners* was so successful. He explained that he could provide a lot of complicated reasons, but that they all came down to one: "It's funny." He was right to an extent, but he underestimated the impact of his own work. This show was more than simply "funny."

It dramatized the underside of the American dream, the life of working class folks who survived week to week, month to month, scraping by, with little hope of a change in fortune.

The Kramdens didn't live in an attractive apartment or in a suburban house with a picket fence and a lawn. They lived on the second floor of a tenement.

The husband didn't work in "the office" or relax at "the club." He knocked himself out driving a bus.

The wife didn't wear heels and jewelry to vacuum the house. She dressed drably without adornment.

Their pleasures were few. Their fears and unfulfilled dreams were many.

WALKING DISTANCE

All that sustained them was love for each other and affection for their friends, and in every show both were tested, sometimes to the breaking point. But somehow both survived.

After the original run of *The Honeymooners* ended in September, 1956, Gleason, as indicated earlier, shut down production, believing that the level of excellence could not be maintained. Subsequently he returned to his original variety hour format, including more episodes of *The Honeymooners*, but ratings were not strong, and that show ended. He next turned to Broadway in the musical *Take Me Along*, for which he earned a Tony Award for Best Actor, an ironic prize for a man who did so much in television but never won an Emmy.

In 1962 his next major foray was another variety show, *The American Scene Magazine*, shot in Miami Beach, Florida, "the sun and fun capital of the world." During its years Gleason did all he could to burnish his image as a man of massive appetites and lavish pleasures. The catch phrase he used to reflect his view of his life was one he borrowed from the character he played in the film *Papa's Delicate Condition*: "How sweet it is!" Gleason himself was awarded the nickname "The Great One" by Orson Welles, and spent the rest of his life living up to that sobriquet, spending money as gaudily as possible and publicly luxuriating with the best scotch, the best food, the most elegant clothes, and the most beautiful women.

The Honeymooners returned in several formats, notably in a musical version during the 1960s. The plot sent the Kramdens and the Nortons on a world tour, and once again Art Carney played opposite Gleason, but this time Sheila MacRae enacted Alice and Jane Kean took on Trixie. The characters were revived for the final time in four "specials" during 1976-78. Finally in 1985 Gleason released a collection of older *Honeymooners* sketches from his vault, and they were publicized as "The Lost Episodes."

Gleason's most profitable movie success was as Sheriff Buford T. Justice in the *Smokey and the Bandit* series, but he also showed himself to be a fine dramatic actor. Drawing on his skill at pool, he played the dapper Minnesota Fats in *The Hustler* (1961), for which he earned an Oscar nomination. He also starred as a desperate fight manager in the movie version of Rod Serling's *Requiem for a Heavyweight* (1962) and as a cynical sergeant opposite Steve McQueen in *Soldier in the Rain* (1963). He received more strong reviews performing opposite Laurence Olivier in the HBO television special *Mr. Halpern and Mr. Johnson* (1983). His final movie was *Nothing in Common* (1987), in which he enacted an embittered father forced to rely on

The Honeymooners and All in the Family

his estranged son, played by Tom Hanks. During the filming Gleason was terminally ill, and although he kept his medical reports private, he understood the gravity of his condition. He died on June 24, 1987.

On *The Honeymooners*, Alice and Ralph Kramden did not have children, but in a sense they were the progenitors of many characters, including Archie Bunker. Indeed, during the early stages of the development of *All in the Family*, Jackie Gleason, still under contract to CBS, was considered for the role, but producer Norman Lear controlled the script and offered it to ABC. That network turned down two separate pilots, but a third ironically ended up on CBS. This script became the first one aired and featured the final cast.

The opening night broadcast on January 12, 1971 was preceded by an introduction:

> The program you are about to see is *All in the Family*. It seeks to throw a humorous spotlight on our frailties, prejudices, and concerns. By making them a source of laughter, we hope to show—in a mature fashion—just how absurd they are.

From that moment, the series would grapple with every social issue: race, war, sex, crime, menopause, abortion, rape, religion, death, and more. No subject was outside its bounds.

The cast was headed by Carroll O'Connor, a veteran of New York theater and numerous television series. He often played an upper-class villain, but here he was cast as Archie Bunker (originally "Archie Justice"), a member of the middle-class and, more important, a shameless bigot. Yet he never thought of himself as such, only as a loyal American who articulated traditional conservative values. What made O'Connor's performance so impressive was that his version of Archie was pained most of all by changes in his world. Thus the audience understood him to be not inherently cruel or hateful but a man struggling to maintain beliefs that both he and the audience knew were headed to extinction. One side note. Producer Lear initially offered the role to Mickey Rooney, but the veteran star could not stomach Archie's values and feared both controversy and failure.

Jean Stapleton was cast as Edith Bunker. She was also a Broadway veteran, notably in hit musicals like *Damn Yankees, Bells Are Ringing,* and *Funny Girl*. She also appeared extensively on television, and in one episode of *The Defenders*, "The Hidden Jungle," acted opposite her future television husband, Carroll O'Connor.

WALKING DISTANCE

Rob Reiner, son of Carl Reiner, the creator of *The Dick Van Dyke Show*, played Archie's son-in-law and nemesis, Mike Stivic, disparaged notoriously by Archie as "Meathead." Sally Struthers played Gloria, Edith and Archie's daughter. Until this show, her most notable appearance had been opposite Jack Nicholson in the film *Five Easy Pieces*.

In another piece of casting irony, the part of Gloria was nearly given to Penny Marshall, sister of writer-director Garry Marshall. Soon after *All in the Family* began, she married Rob Reiner, so the show might have had a real-life husband and wife playing the young couple. Reiner and Marshall were divorced several years later, and she went on to star in *The Odd Couple* (opposite Reiner in one episode) and *Laverne and Shirley*. Both Reiner and Marshall have since enjoyed outstanding careers as movie directors.

The script was based on the British television comedy *Till Death Do Us Part*, a far more vitriolic entity than its American counterpart. The other main influence on producer Lear was his own father, who regularly deprecated Lear's mother with one of Archie's catchphrases, "stifle yourself." Lear's father also dismissed his son as "the laziest white man I ever saw." Fortunately the relationship between Archie and Edith was not nearly as antagonistic as that between Lear's parents. Although Archie regularly grew impatient with Edith, often because of her generosity towards individuals for whom he had no tolerance, she demonstrated remarkable forbearance with him. Indeed, her affection assured the audience that even if Archie said and did things that we despised, other qualities redeemed him.

Although the tension between Archie and his son-in-law Mike initially seemed simple, it was actually subtle and complicated. After Mike married Gloria and resumed attending college, the couple lived with Archie and Edith. Adding to the level of discomfort was that while Archie was conservative, even reactionary on certain issues, Mike was an unashamed liberal. Archie was also prone to comic malapropisms, while Mike spoke with a more sophisticated vocabulary. Yet just as Archie was set in his views, so Mike, too, often refused to tolerate disagreement. His liberal perspectives generally reflected the spirit of the show, but his overbearing manner could make him uncongenial, and this tendency sometimes created conflict with Gloria, who rejected many of her father's opinions, but still loved him. Gloria also recognized another of Mike's less admirable traits: he could be a male chauvinist of the first order. On one occasion, for instance, he needed an appendectomy, but was reluctant to let a woman surgeon operate. And on a night when Gloria and Mike were home alone for the evening, his male ego led him to reject her sexual advances.

The Honeymooners and *All in the Family*

But the episode that revealed the most about Mike is "The Games Bunkers Play." With Archie away, Mike brings out an encounter-therapy board game to share with family and neighbors. To his shock, he finds himself criticized as intolerant and preachy, and when he rejects such criticism, he evokes accusations of immaturity. Even his African American neighbor, Lionel, whom Mike considers his best friend, suggests that Mike should treat him as an ordinary pal, not as a representative of an entire race. When Edith suggests what Mike judges to be the most unfair criticism, that he ought to be more understanding of Archie, Mike storms from the room. In the kitchen, however, Edith counsels him with the innate humanity that audiences loved. Mike grouses that Archie hates him, but Edith insists that Archie is actually jealous. At first Mike refuses to listen, but Edith asserts herself: "You *will* listen!" She explains that Archie will never be more than he is, but that Mike has a limitless future awaiting him: "If you really was smarter than Archie, you'd be smart enough to not let him see that you're smarter than him." Moments later, when Archie returns from Kelcey's Bar, Mike embraces him: "I understand." In sum, Mike may have advocated what the writers implied was the proper side of most issues, but he was hardly a paragon. The show was never that obvious.

"Judging Books By Covers," first broadcast on February 9, 1971, was the fourth episode of *All in the Family* to air. By now, the country overflowed with editorials, sermons, and articles about the program, particularly Archie's casual use of epithets like "chink" and "spic." Indeed, for many viewers Archie's tirades against one ethnic group or another remain the most memorable aspect of the show. This particular episode, however, concerns homosexuality, a subject that was sensational in its time and which still resonates.

The episode, written by Lear and Burt Styler, was directed by John Rich, who worked extensively on *The Dick Van Dyke Show*. The story begins with Mike studying and Gloria preparing lunch, stereotypes still operative at this stage of the series. At Gloria's request, though, Mike gladly helps set the table, a traditionally "feminine" task. Yet when Gloria asks for assistance in the kitchen, but warns Michael not to grab "any samples," he responds, "Only one sample I want to grab," and reaches for her. Gloria in turn giggles and scurries back to the kitchen, with Michael close behind. He therefore comes off as a "normal" heterosexual male, a familiar image in the series, but a subtle contrast to two other males in this episode.

Archie and Edith then come downstairs, with Edith bemoaning that every time the church conducts an old clothes drive, she must lie that "My husband doesn't have any old clothes." Archie, however, feels no shame: "That's what's wrong with this country today: too many handouts." With one line he dismisses all charity. The line is facile, but it establishes the parameters of Archie's bigotry, which at this point needed to be clarified.

His temperament is further revealed when he notices the foods Mike and Gloria have laid out, including "fine cashews" and "clam dip." Archie not only resents the extra money spent on lunch for one of Mike's and Gloria's friends, but wants to know the identity of this special guest: "The Duke of Windsor?" Mike reluctantly admits the truth: Roger is coming. Archie's response is blunt: "Roger the *fairy*?" The directness of this accusation is unsettling even today. After Archie adds that Roger is "as queer as a four-dollar bill," Mike attempts to burst the prejudice: "Just because a guy is sensitive, and he's an intellectual, and he wears glasses, you make him out a queer." Archie's retort is a characteristic conviction: "A guy who wears glasses is a four-eyes. A guy who's a fag is a queer." When Archie adds that Roger is obviously a "pansy," then seeks Edith's affirmation, she confesses that she is not "an expert on flowers." Both Archie's and Edith's comments suggest that they have not contemplated precisely what homosexuality is. Indeed, when Michael asserts that laws in England have changed, so that now "whatever two consenting adults do in private is their own business," Archie shows no understanding of what that behavior might be. Instead he offers a nonsensical precept: "England is a fag country." In fact, he continues, British society is "based on a certain kind of fagdom." The last word is bizarre, but curiously clever, suggesting that Archie possesses a measure of wit. So does his imitation of what he judges to be characteristic English mannerisms, such as pulling a handkerchief from one's sleeve or leaning on an umbrella. Nevertheless, as A. J. Aronstein clarifies in his insightful analysis of this episode, in Archie's mind "sexual identity has almost *nothing* to do with sex: it has to do with aesthetics—with adopting a certain style or sensibility" (Aronstein). Thus despite his veneer of worldliness, Archie is naïve about this matter and, as the series gradually suggested, many others.

Archie's last line before Roger's entrance is intriguing. After Gloria warns him to be "good," Archie smirks: "If I can't be good, I'll be careful." This expression usually invokes one of two meanings: first, that the individual will resist unwelcome advances, and, second, that the individual will control desires. Archie obviously has the first meaning in mind, although

The Honeymooners and *All in the Family*

why Roger might judge him worth pursuing is unclear. But even the possibility that the second meaning applies is humorous.

When Roger enters, he does not necessarily fulfill our expectations, because he is not overtly effeminate. (He is played by Tony Geary, soon to star as Luke Spencer on *General Hospital*.) Rather, with his ascot and sharply tailored jacket, he looks flamboyant or perhaps "continental." Nor does his voice have qualities usually judged to be effeminate. True, his register is high, but what confirms Archie's judgment is Roger's vocabulary, which includes "super," "fabulous," "stunning," and "exhilarating." At these descriptions, Archie mumbles to himself, "When is he going to land?" Roger then greets Edith with a two-handed shake. She is taken aback, but in a spirit of fellowship puts her other hand on top of his. Archie, however, resists: "One is enough." He does not want to commit any action that might brand him.

Archie then asks whether Roger, who has been to Europe, enjoyed any sports there such as "bobsledding," a "manly sport." The image of that competition, which demands that two or four men be bunched together, seems not to have occurred to Archie. Roger explains that bobsledding is not popular in London, to which Archie looks at Mike knowingly: "Your witness."

One extraneous passage deserves comment. As Roger, who's a photographer, presents some pictures he took overseas, Edith reflects that she remains fascinated by how people in pictures appear frozen in time, but that right after the picture is taken, they move on. As Archie listens to her disquisition, his numb expression tells all. So does his comment at the end of her comment: "You're a pip, Edith. You know what? You're a regular 'Edna St. Louis Millay.'" Writers Lear and Styler must have enjoyed coming up with that turn of phrase.

Finally Archie can bear no more and prepares to visit Kelcey's bar and his friend Steve, who, we soon learn, owns a photography store. How Archie knows that Steve will be there is unclear, but the claim establishes that Archie values male camaraderie, although he is oblivious to the possibility that such bonding has other overtones. He leaves with a satirical expression of parting: "It's been a charming interlude."

In Kelcey's bar, Archie huddles over beers with three other men. One is Steve (played by the ruggedly handsome Philip Carey, a movie veteran who from 1979–2007 played Asa Buchanan on *One Life to Live*). The other two denizens are familiar character actors: Bill Halop (once a member of "The Dead End Kids") and Billy Sands (who formerly served in two of television's celebrated military units: Bilko's motor pool and McHale's PT crew). The bartender, whom we do not yet see, is another member of the "McHale's" team: Bob Hastings, who played stuffy Lt. Carpenter. Right now Archie and his buddies discuss economics, but soon the conversation turns to the glories of American individualism, one example of "a God-given right." That other activities might fall into this category does not strike these fellows, but we are aware of additional implications.

As the men discuss elementary economics (the subject Michael studied at the start of the episode), Steve shares Archie's views. But when the topic changes to a new Swedish movie, one that, like so many others, Archie characterizes as "sheer porno-*graphy*," Steve drifts away. Archie assumes that the subject bores Steve, who as a good-looking bachelor must enjoy an enviable heterosexual life: "You don't have to go to no movies to see your Wandas, eh Steve?"

A side note. As the two men stand and talk, Steve pops peanuts into his mouth, and one drops to the floor, but the taping of the show continues. The realistic moment helps maintain believability. We also note that Steve is dressed more fashionably and colorfully than the others.

At the table Archie cannot resist trying to ingratiate himself with Steve, whom he clearly idolizes. Earlier Archie suggested that football used to be "rougher" and "tougher," an assertion that Steve dismisses, but his denial only encourages Archie to express his envy more directly: "How do you keep yourself in such great shape? . . . I mean, look at your shoulders and all o' that." That such flattery could be interpreted as a sexual invitation passes Archie completely. Meanwhile we wonder whether his praise reflects Archie's own desire to be younger and stronger (how Archie himself would probably interpret his words), or a subconscious desire to be *with* Steve. The latter's amused expression reflects that he perceives both possibilities.

Steve's revelation that he practices archery surprises Archie, who obviously considers the sport less than masculine. But Steve assures him that "It's good for the arms and shoulders," then jabs Archie twice. The blows hurt, but Archie seems almost aroused by Steve's strength. That feeling quickly sours, though, when Mike and Roger enter the bar. Archie is disgusted by the presence of his son-in-law and his pal "Tinker Bell," but distaste turns to astonishment when Roger and Steve turn out to be friends. The two chat about photographic equipment that Steve sold him, and Archie finds himself not only left out, but also confused.

The Honeymooners and *All in the Family*

Kelsey, the bartender, then takes Mike aside to ask whether Roger is straight. Initially Mike is annoyed at Kelcey's attitude, but bar owner explains that since Roger seems be so "buddy-buddy with Steve . . . "? Mike still fails to see the implications, so Kelcey explains in an exaggerated macho New York accent: "Don't get me wrong. I don't mind Steve . . . Besides, he don't . . . *camp it up*. And he don't bring in none of his friends." Kelsey adds that he doesn't want his place "to turn into no . . . *hangout*." At this revelation that Steve is gay, Mike can only stare, just as Archie did. The liberal and the conservative are both taken aback.

The second act begins with the Edith, Gloria, Mike, and Roger at the dinner table. Roger is about to leave when Archie hurries in, eager to watch a special called "Great Fights of the Century." Roger disclaims any interest in "pugilism," a statement that bewilders Archie: "Who's talking about pugilism? I asked you to watch the fights." As Roger leaves, Archie calls Mike over and whispers that he should just open the window and "we'll all watch Roger fly out." We are aware of what Mike knows, but he restrains himself.

At this moment the writers bring in a seemingly irrelevant distraction, but one which hits the hub of the episode. Archie claims that nothing Mike can tell him will shock him, but Gloria challenges her father. She sets a chair by the wall, steps three steps back, lowers her head against the wall, lifts the chair, and stands straight. She explains that women can complete this simple maneuver, but that men cannot. Michael tries and affirms her statement, then invites Archie to do his best. He naturally fails, then shouts that the chair must be rigged. While he retrieves another chair, Edith comes over and completes the stunt. Now Archie is furious: how can Edith do something that he cannot?

Mike explains that women are built differently, a reality that Archie claims that he has known for a long time. Then he asks who showed everyone this "dumb gag." When Mike reveals that Roger is the source, Archie is reassured: "If a man can't do it, I would imagine that your friend Roger Bell can." At this insult, Mike can no longer control himself: "You know who could lift that chair, Arch? . . . and prance and flit all over this room with it? Your friend Steve." This assertion infuriates Archie. Until now he has accepted social criticism by young people: "You're sick. You need help. All this pinko stuff, well, that's all right . . . Their wide open sex any time of the night or day, for no reason at all. All right, that's your submissive society." Archie's use of the word "submissive," with its sexual connotations, may be for him a mere malapropism, but no doubt Lear and Styler knew what they were doing. Moreover, as Aronstein points out, "one theme of this episode is Archie's apparent jealousy that everyone is getting action with anonymous partners, except him" (Aronstein). Now, however, Mike has gone too far, "besmearing the name of a great linebacker. A man, I mean a real man."

Now we see the point of the chair trick, which raises questions that underlie all the conflicts that have been articulated in the last twenty minutes: what do we mean by a "man"? What do we mean by "masculine" and "feminine"?

Back at the bar, the same four men are watching the boxing program to which Archie was tuned. Inexplicably they cheer the fighters, even though the outcome is known. After all, as Steve comments, "the knockout isn't until the tenth round." After the bout, the others depart, leaving Archie to resist Steve's playful boxing moves: "The law says those mitts of yours are lethal weapons." Instead Archie once again challenges Steve to arm wrestle for the drinks, and Steve easily pins him. "Beeyoutiful," is Archie's reaction.

Then he raises the issue that has ostensibly been bothering him: that young people today show "no respect for the old institutions." When Steve asks for specifics, Archie hints at his real concern: "sports, sportsmanship, guts, guns. Things that separate the sexes." Steve remains noncommittal, so Archie asks to arm-wrestle once more, then zeroes in on Roger: "You're a man of the world. You must know that this kid is kind of a lad-dee-dah."

Steve remains calm: "Is that what Mike thinks of Roger?" Then he smiles, and the following sequence overflows with tension, as we wonder how Steve will react to the implication that he is gay.

Archie is too embarrassed to state directly what Mike told him. Instead he suggests another arm wrestling contest, but Steve is not deterred: "What *does* Mike think?" We feel him almost asking to have his secret exposed.

Here the two men grip hands almost sensually, and Archie, eager to learn the truth, yet fearful, skirts the issue: "Well, for one thing, he thinks that friend of his Roger is straight." But the next question is impossible for Archie to articulate: "And for another thing . . . he thinks that you . . . I can't even say it . . ."

Steve pauses, then grins at Archie. "He's right, Arch."

Archie's eyes open wide: "Heh?"

"He's right." Here Steve slams Archie's hand against the table.

For a moment the two men stare at each other. Yet Archie still cannot accept the truth: "You mean he's right about his friend Roger?"

Steve still smiles: "About everything."

The Honeymooners and All in the Family

During the pauses, we feel Steve's mixture of anguish and relief at outing himself. At the same time, we feel Archie's pain at having another illusion shattered: "Aw, come off it, guy."

Steve explains further: "Arch, how long have you known me? Ten, twelve years? In all that time, did I ever mention a woman?"

Archie thinks he understands: "Well, I know, but bachelors... they're always acting kind of private."

"Exactly," says Steve.

With the evidence directly in front of him, Archie still denies it: "C'mon, you big clown, get outta here," so Steve lets Archie off the hook: "Have it your own way, Arch. The truth is in the eye of the beholder, anyway."

He stands and gives an extra-firm punch to Archie's shoulder, but, more important, leaves him befuddled.

Archie ponders what he has just heard and felt: "Well, if that's the punch of a fruit..." He then dismisses the possibility and leaves. Throughout this moment, O'Connor's range of facial expression is brilliant.

In the epilogue, so often cut from syndicated versions of this show, we see Michael and Gloria back home demonstrating the chair problem to a short-haired figure wearing jeans and an athletic jacket, and answering to the name Jerry. As Archie enters and watches, the figure lifts up the chair successfully, just as Edith and Gloria did. Now Archie is convinced once again that the furniture is rigged. When that figure turns around, however, we see that it is a young woman. Archie stares at her, then stalks away mumbling: "These days you can't bet on nothin.'"

If any line may be said to sum up Archie's character, this one serves well. The impact of this particular episode, however, reached all the way to the White House, where President Nixon was heard to say on his notorious tapes: "That was awful. It made a fool out of a great man." We must ask who the "great man" is. Was the President talking about Archie? Or was he talking about Steve, who doesn't come off at all like a fool? Or in Nixon's eyes, was any homosexual a fool?

The answer doesn't matter. What does is how a television show could provoke comment from so high a source.

At the start of this book, I suggested that the most influential program in the history of television is *The Twilight Zone*. If any other show may legitimately lay claim to that title, the show would be *All in the Family*. Other programs, including some discussed in this book, demanded that the scripts conform to principles of reality. *All in the Family,* though, broke all the rules and established a new one:

> Before *All in the Family*, moral questions comfortably found their place in TV sitcoms, but only when readily answered by unwavering moral law . . . Real issues, like real people, are complex, and serious subjects dare not be treated too simply for fear the subjects themselves might seem trivialized or diminished. (McCrohan 182)

"Judging Books By Covers" reflects this innovative tone that dominated the first season, when critical response was immediate and strong. It generally fell into two camps. One held that hearing venal opinions articulated by someone like Archie guaranteed that his ideas would appear ridiculous. The other argued that because Archie was innately likeable, he reinforced the bigotry of those who agreed with him.

The controversy remains as yet unresolved, as it does for all works of art that make us face unpleasant truths.

Where *All in the Family* broke additional ground was in dramatizing the most intimate aspects of life. Some of these had been dramatized on other programs, but never with such gritty realism. In one show Mike suffers impotence; in another Edith experiences menopause. These physical difficulties were painful for the characters, yet as dramatized by skillful writers and actors still inspired laughter. The Bunkers' neighbors also contributed powerfully. Early on, Lionel's family, the Jeffersons, moved next door, and the antagonism between Archie and Lionel's uncle and father led to bitter, yet wild confrontations about race. Later Irene and Frank Lorenzo moved nearby. He loved to cook and she was handy with tools, just two of their attributes that left Archie flummoxed.

Sometimes, though, the program broached subjects that defied any possibility of humor. During the first season, Gloria suffered a miscarriage, a tragedy that permitted Archie to reveal genuine compassion. During a later season, a swastika was painted on Archie's door, and a member of the Hebrew Defense Association, trying to protect Archie, was blown up in his car. Later Gloria was attacked on the street. In a two-part episode set during Edith's birthday, she was almost raped. In a later episode, her cross-dressing friend, whose life was once saved by Archie, was beaten to death during Christmas. In a shocking revelation to Mike, Archie recounted the frightful abuse he suffered at the hands of his father. Finally Edith herself died.

Such material would be powerful no matter who the victims might be. But when they were characters whom we had known for years and come to love, our outrage was intensified almost beyond endurance. At such moments, *All in the Family* ceased being a comedy. Yet ironically its frank language, mature themes, and bold characters opened possibilities for other comedies like M*A*S*H and Barney Miller up to Arrested Development and others that have grappled with issues of import. We still laugh, but after *All in the Family* we never laughed in innocence.

All in the Family and its successor, *Archie Bunker's Place* (Archie took over management of Kelcey's bar), ran in various forms from 1971–1983. During that time it remained one of the top-rated programs, as the character of Archie endured for 307 episodes over thirteen years. When the show was cancelled without what O'Connor judged to be a proper send-off, he vowed never to work in television again. Years later, however, he enjoyed success on the television version of the film *In the Heat of the Night*, in which he played Sheriff Bill Gillespie, and maintained substantial control over scripts and other aspects of production. That series also featured his son, Hugh O'Connor, whose own life turned tragic when he committed suicide after battling drug addiction. Carroll O'Connor spent the remainder of his life promoting the cause of drug prevention. He died June 21, 2001.

After Jean Stapleton left *All in the family*, she returned to theater and movies, and also toured in a one-woman play about Eleanor Roosevelt. Stapleton was offered the lead in the program *Murder, She Wrote*, but declined, and the part went to Angela Lansbury, who played it for twelve seasons. Stapleton died on May 31, 2013.

Norman Lear went on to produce some of the most popular and controversial shows America has ever seen. Some were offshoots of *All in the Family*, such as *The Jeffersons* and *Maude*. Others explored an entirely different vein, such as *Mary Hartman, Mary Hartman*. As of this writing, Lear is ninety, the recipient of countless honors, and a man whose his legacy as one of the most daring and innovative minds in television history is beyond question.

As for *The Honeymooners* and *All in the Family*, together they covered almost three decades of American life, and in reruns they keep those years alive. Both dramatized a segment of American society often ignored on television, and both produced stories and characters with extraordinary humor and a huge dose of heart.

Epilogue

In 2009 I published the memoir *Classroom Virtuoso: Recollections of a Life in Learning* (Rowman & Littlefield). In it I recall my experiences in all kinds of education: my brother's tutelage that helped me learn about the U.S. Presidents; my lifelong study of the violin; my classes from elementary grades through graduate work, and my teaching English at prep school and college. I also recount my efforts as a playwright and an actor.

What I never discuss is my youthful devotion to television, and I hope this book compensates for that omission. The writing has also made me realize that ever since I was old enough to turn on a set, I've pondered matters of plot, language, character, and theme. Thus the activities to which I've devoted my professional life seem almost inevitable.

I'll conclude by citing one surprising pleasure of seeing these programs from decades back: finding various actors in unlikely contexts. A few of these men and women would become stars. Many, however, were character players whose names would never become familiar to most viewers, but whose faces remain well known. I've mentioned a couple, and I could name hundreds more. They played police officers and criminals, nurses and teachers, clerks and secretaries, cowboys and judges, and surgeons and soldiers. I enjoy also seeing actors switch roles: on one show they're doctor and patient; on another they're bartender and customer. Sometimes I come across actors who years before were in the same movie or television series, but not in scenes together, and I speculate about the stories they shared. Sometimes I see actors in one show who at that time were otherwise unconnected, but who in a few years would co-star on another program. Did they remember the production in which they both appeared? As an actor myself, I cannot help but wonder what life was like for these performers, who didn't necessarily make much money, but who worked on show after show, hoping for a big break that might or might not come.

WALKING DISTANCE

Now I have the opportunity to experience these moments again on DVD and the web. The pictures are clearer than ever, the episodes are complete and uninterrupted by commercials, and, best of all, I can rewind and watch as many times as I want.

Like Martin Sloan, I again "hear the voices and the laughter of the people and the places" of my past.

Works Cited

Allen, Woody. *Annie Hall* by Woody Allen and Marshall Brickman in *Four Films of Woody Allen*. New York: Random House, 1982.
Anton, Michael. "Rod Serling's Revenge." *National Review Online*. October 7, 2009.
Aronstein, A.J. "*All in the Family* and the First Gay Sitcom Character." http://splitsider.com. May 30, 2012.
Brevelle, Linda. "Rod Serling's Final Interview." Originally appeared in *Writers' Digest Magazine*, 1976. Reproduced inwww.nmreview.com, 2000.
Brower, Neal. *Mayberry 101: Behind the Scenes of a TV Classic*. Winston-Salem: John F. Blair, 1998.
Carrazeé, Alan and Jean-Luc Putheaud with Alex J. Geairns. "*The Avengers*" *Companion*. London: Titan Books, 1997.
Conlon, Christopher. "The Many Fathers of Martin Sloan." Originally appeared in *Filmfax Magazine*, Dec. 2000-Jan 2001. Reproduced in rodserling.com/msloan.htm.
Cornell, Paul, Martin Day, and Keith Topping. "*The Avengers*" *Dossier*. London: Virgin Books, 1998.
Crescenti Peter and Bob Columbe. *The Official "Honeymooners" Treasury*. New York: Perigree Books, 1990.
Fish, Stanley. *The Fugitive in Flight: Faith Liberalism and Law in a Class TV Show*. Philadelphia: University of Pennsylvania Press, 2011.
Garner, James and Jon Winokur. The Garner Files. New York: Simon & Schuster, 2011.
Get Smart: The Complete Series. DVD. HBO Video, 2008.
Grams, Martin, Jr. "*The Twilight Zone*": *Unlocking the Door to a Television Classic* Churchville, MD: OTR Publishing, 2008.
Green, Joey. *The "Get Smart" Handbook*. New York: Collier Books, 1993.
Kelly, Richard. *The Andy Griffith Show*. Winston-Salem: John F. Blair, 1981.
Mannion, Lance. "How Hero-worshipping Rob Petrie Ruined My Life." http://lancemannion.typepad.com/lance_mannion.24/01/10.
McCrohan, Donna. *Archie & Edith, Mike & Gloria*. New York: Workman Publishing, 1987.
Metz, Rick. *The Great TV Sitcom Book*. New York: Richard Marek Publishers, 1980.
Miller, Toby. *The Avengers*. London: BFI Publishing, 1997.
"Of All the Shows, Which One is Considered The Best?" www.philsilversshow.com/BestShow. No date or author given.
Robertson, Ed. *Maverick: Legend of the West*. 2nd ed., 2012. Originally published in Los Angeles by Pomegranate Press, 1994.

Works Cited

Serling, Rod. "Walking Distance." In *As Timeless As Infinity: The Complete "Twilight Zone" Scripts of Rod Serling*, vol. 2. Edited by Tony Albarella. Gauntlet Publications: Colorado Springs, CO, 2005.

Waldron, Vince, *The Official "Dick Van Dyke Show" Book*. New York: Hyperion, 1994.

Zicree, Mark Scott. *The Twilight Zone Companion*. New York: Bantam Books, 1982.

Index

2001: A Space Odyssey, 7
The $64,000 Question, 109

Abbott and Costello, 70
"Aboard the Orient Express," *Get Smart*, 112
Absolutely Fabulous, 107
Adams, Don, 108, 109–110, 112, 119
Adventures of Superman, 1
Aherne, Brian, 20
Alcoa Presents, 36
All in the Family, 121, 123, 135–145
All in the Family, "Judging Books By Covers." *See* "Judging Books By Covers," *All in the Family*
"All the Scared Rabbits," *The Fugitive*, 66
Allen, Gracie, 111
Allen, Steve, 4, 37, 108
Allen, Woody, 70
Amazing Stories, 8
The American Scene Magazine, 134
Amsterdam, Morey, 72
The Andy Griffith Show, 13, 69, 71, 84–92, 108, 124
The Andy Griffith Show, "Man in a Hurry." *See* "Man in a Hurry," *The Andy Griffith Show*
"Andy on Trial," *The Andy Griffith Show*, 85
Apollo 13, 13
Archie Bunker's Place, 145
Are You Being Served?, 100
Armstrong, R. G., 66
Arnaz, Desi, x, 75
Arness, James, 46
Arnie, Rosen, 29

Arnold, Tom, 42
Aronstein, A. J., 138, 142
Arrested Development, 145
Arthur, Robert Alan, 8
As Timeless as Infinity: The Complete "Twilight Zone" Scripts of Rod Serling, 9
Autry, Gene, 44, 45
The Avengers, 94, 95, 96, 97, 98–105, 106, 107, 119
The Avengers, "Escape in Time." *See* "Escape in Time," *The Avengers*
*Avengers*land, 98, 101

"Baby Fat," *The Dick Van Dyke Show*, 74–75, 76–82
Babylon 5, 6
Backus, Jim, ix
Bad Day at Black Rock, 36
The Bad Seed, 49
Baker, Diane, 23
Ball, Lucille, x, 75
Ballantine, Carl, 38
The Bank Dick, 26
Barney Miller, 145
Barr, Byron, 20
Barr, Rosanne, 7
Bartlett, Juanita, 57
Bat Masterson, 47
Bavier, Frances, 84
Beat the Clock, 4
Beaumont, Charles, 7, 13
A Beautiful Mind, 13
Beckett, Samuel, 19, 30
Bells Are Ringing, 135
Belson, Jerry, 74, 78

151

Index

Bendix, William, 124
Benny, Jack, 38, 83
Berle, Milton, 27, 35, 74
The Beverly Hillbillies, 91
Bewitched, 20
"Big Max Calvada," *The Dick Van Dyke Show*, 83
Bilko, 24–36, 42, 140. See also *The Phil Silvers Show*
"The Black Ferris," 20
Blackman, Honor, 96–97, 106
Blue Velvet, 7
Bogart, Humphrey, 115
Bonnie and Clyde, 111
Boone, Richard, 46–47
Borgnine, Ernest, 25, 26, 36–37, 42
Bowles, Peter, 102
Bradbury, Ray, 13, 20
Brando, Marlon, 49
Brewster, Diane, 53
Bronson, Charles, 7
Brooks, Mel, 108, 109, 111, 112, 119
Brower, Neal, 89
Brown, Cindy Lou, 54
Brown, Johnny Mack, 44
Buck, Henry, 109
"Buddy Sorrell, Man and Boy," *The Dick Van Dyke Show*, 83
Buffy the Vampire, 6
Bullock, Harvey, 90, 91
Bumgarner, James. See Garner, James
Burnett, Carol, 7
Burnette, Smiley, 45
Burns, George, 111
Burr, Raymond, ix
Burrows, Abe, 78
Buttram, Pat, 45
Bye, Bye, Birdie, 71–72

Caesar, Sid, 71, 72, 74, 108
Caesar's Hour, 71, 108
The Caine Mutiny Court Martial, 49
Car 54, Where are You, 35
Carell, Steve, 119
Carey, Philip, 139
Carillo, Leo, 45
Carney, Art, 125, 127, 134
The Carol Burnett Show, 42

Carson, Johnny, 4, 72, 112
Casablanca, 111
"Casablanca," *Get Smart*, 111–118
"The Case of Harry Speakup," *Bilko*, 29
Catch-22, 37
Cavalcade of Stars, 124, 125, 127
Cavella, Carol, 111
Cavella, Joseph C., 111
Champion, Gower, 72
Charmed, 6
Chase, David, 7
Chayevsky, Paddy, 8
Cheyenne, 47
"The Church in the Wildwood," *The Andy Griffith Show*, 88
The Cisco Kid, 45
Citizen Kane, 9
Clark, Harry, 33
"The Classic Thirty-Nine," *The Honeymooners*, 125, 126, 133
Classroom Virtuoso: Recollections of a Life in Learning, 147
Clemens, Brian, 98
"Coast-to-Coast Big Mouth," *The Dick Van Dyke Show*, 77
Coates, Phyllis, 2
Cocoon, 13
College Bowl, 4
Collins, Ray, ix
Colman, Ronald, 118
Columbo, 92
Come Fill the Cup, 20
Conlon, Christopher, 20
Connery, Sean, 49
Conrad, William, 60
Convy, Bert, 23
Conway, Tim, 27, 37–38, 41, 42
Cool Hand Luke, 26
Cooper, Gladys, 7
"Corner of Hell," *The Fugitive*, 65
"The Correct Way to Kill," *The Avengers*, 106
Corsaut, Anita, 86
"The Court Martial," *Bilko*, 24, 29–34
Cover Girl, 27
Crawford, Joan, 100
Cronkite, Walter, 72

Index

Dallas, 67
Daly, James, 19
Damn Yankees, 135
Dana, Bill, 108, 110
The Danny Thomas Show, 71, 84, 108
Davis, Bette, 100
Day, Doris, 52
Deacon, Richard, 72, 76
"The Dead End Kids," 139
Dean, James, 109
"Dear Diary," *McHale's Navy*, 24, 38–41
Death of a Salesman, 121, 122, 123, 126, 127
DeCaprio, Al, 29
Deep Impact, 7
Deep Space Nine, 6
The Defenders, 135
Dehner, John, 50, 52, 54, 57
Denver, Bob, ix
Detour, 60
Diagnosis: Murder, 92
Diamond, Selma, 72
The Dick Van Dyke Show, 7, 69, 70, 71–84, 92, 108, 124, 136, 137
The Dick Van Dyke Show, "Baby Fat." See "Baby Fat," *The Dick Van Dyke Show*
The Dirty Dozen, 111
The Doris Day Show, 52
"Double Exposure," *Columbo*, 92
Doyle Lonnegan, 52
Dr. No, 94, 111
Duck Soup, 94
Duvall, Robert, 7

Ecuyer, Lee, 31, 32, 33
Emhardt, Robert, 87
ER, 42
Eraserhead, 7
Erdman, Richard, 80
"Escape in Time," *The Avengers*, 98–105
"The Eye of the Beholder," *The Twilight Zone*, 5

A Face in the Crowd, 93
Faye, Herbie, 28
Faye, Joey, 30, 31

Feldon, Barbara, 95, 109, 110, 111, 114, 117, 118, 119
Feydaux, 70
Fields, W. C., 26, 37
Fiennes, Ralph, 107
Fink, Mike, 2
Finn, Herbert, 126
Fish, Stanley, 59, 62, 65
Five Easy Pieces, 136
Fleming, Ian, 94
Flippen, Jay C., 73
The Flying Dutchman (Wagner), 46
Flynn, Joe, 37, 38, 41, 42
Fonda, Henry, 49
Foote, Horton, 8
Forbidden Planet, 49
Ford, Harrison, 68
Ford, Paul, 25, 29
"The Forget-Me-Knot," *The Avengers*, 107
Foster, Ron, 36
Foulger, Byron, 12
Francis, Anne, 7
Fraser, Elizabeth, 34
Frayn, Michael, 70
French, Victor, 109
Fritzell, James, 86
From Here to Eternity, 36
The Fugitive, x, 43, 44, 58–68, 111
The Fugitive, "Nightmare at Northoak." See "Nightmare at Northoak," *The Fugitive*
The Fugitive in Flight: Faith Liberalism, and Law in a Classic TV Show, 59
A Funny Thing Happened on the Way to the Forum, 35

Gable, Clark, 20
"The Games Bunkers Play," *All in the Family*, 137
Garland, Judy, 83
Garner, James, 48–49, 52, 57, 68
Gas, 9
Gautier, Dick, 109
The Gay Sisters, 20
Geary, Tony, 139
General Hospital, 139
Get Smart, 42, 94, 95, 108–120

Index

Get Smart, "Casablanca." See "Casablanca," *Get Smart*
Get Smart Collection, 109, 110, 111
Gibson, Hoot, 44
Gilligan's Island, ix
"The Girl from Auntie," *The Avengers*, 105
Gleason, Jackie, 74, 124–125, 127, 134, 135
Goldfinger, 97, 111
"The Golfer," *The Honeymooners*, 126–133
Gomer Pyle USMC, 108
Gordon, Leo, 54
Gosfield, Maurice, 28
Grable, Betty, 27
Grams, Martin, Jr., 9
"Grand Hung Ball," *The Avengers*, 99
Grant, Cary, 109
Graziano, Rocky, 28
The Great Escape, 111
Great Locomotive Chase, 2
The Great One. See Gleason, Jackie
The Greatest Show on Earth, 58
Green Acres, 91
"Greenbacks Unlimited," *Maverick*, 57
Greenbaum, Everett, 86
Greenstreet, Sidney, 116
Griffith, Andy, 71, 84, 86, 92, 93
Guiding Light, 1
Guilbert, Ann Morgan, 73
"Gun Shy," *Maverick*, 57
Gunsmoke, 46, 52, 57
Guys and Dolls, 78
Gwynne, Fred, 35–36

Hale, Alan, Jr., ix
Hale, Barbara, ix
Hall, Barbara. See Feldon, Barbara
Halop, Bill, 139
Hamilton, John, 2
Hamner, Earl, Jr., 7
Hanks, Tom, 135
Happy Days, 13, 118
Hardy, Oliver, 38, 40
Harry and Tonto, 127
Harry O, 68
Hastings, Bob, 25, 39, 140

Hathaway, Anne, 119
Have Gun--Will Travel, 46–47, 52
Hayes, Gabby, 45
Head of the Family, 71
Healy, Jack, 28
Heller, Joe, 37
Hendry, Ian, 96
Henry, Buck, 108, 119
Hermann, Bernard, 9, 15, 18
Heston, Charlton, 22
Heyes, Douglas, 49
"The Hidden Jungle," *The Defenders*, 135
"The Hidden Tiger," *The Avengers*, 106
Hiken, Nat, 27–28, 29, 35, 36
Hitchcock, Alfred, 9, 58
The Hollywood Reporter, 57
The Honeymooners, x, 121, 123, 124–134, 145
The Honeymooners (musical), 134
"The Honeymooners," *The Calvacade of Stars*, 124, 125
The Honeymooners, "The Golfer." See "The Golfer," *The Honeymooners*
Hopper, Edward, 9
Hopper, Wiliam, ix
Hot in Cleveland, 42
How to Succeed in Business Without Really Trying, 78
Howard, Ronnie, 13, 84
Howell, Arlene, 54
Huggins, Roy, 43, 48, 49, 52, 57, 58, 68
Hugo, Victor, 58–59
Hunt, Gareth, 107
The Hustler, 134

I am Legend, 7
I Love Lucy, x, 75
I Love Trouble, 43
"I Shot an Arrow in the Air," *The Twilight Zone*, 22
In the Heat of the Night, 145
"The Invaders," *The Twilight Zone*, 6
Ironside, 111
"It May Look Like a Walnut," *The Dick Van Dyke Show*, 7
"It's a Good Life," *The Twilight Zone*, 5
It's a Mad, Mad, Mad, Mad World, 35

154

Index

I've Got a Secret, 4

The Jackie Gleason Show, 124
Jacoby, Coleman, 29
Janssen, David, 58, 68, 72
The Jeffersons, 144, 145
Jerome, Stuart, 60
Johnson, George Clayton, 7
"The Joker," *The Avengers*, 106
Jones, Tomy Lee, 68
"Judging Books By Covers," *All in the Family*, 137–144
"Judgment Day," *The Fugitive*, 66

Kallen, Lucille, 72
Karl, Harry, 35
Kazan, Elia, 93
Kean, Jane, 134
Keaton, Buster, 7
Keaton, Diane, 70
Kelly, Gene, 83
Kelly, Jack, 49, 57
Kelly, Nancy, 49
Kelton, Pert, 125
Kennedy, George, 25–26
Kenyon, Sandy, 79
Ketchum, Dave, 109
King, Stephen, 7
"The King Lives?" *Get Smart*, 118
Klugman, Jack, 127
Knotts, Don, 37, 71, 84, 91
Kopell, Bernie, 109
Korman, Harvey, 42
Kramer, Stanley, 35
Krapp's Last Tape, 19
Krish, John, 98
Kubrick, Stanley, 7

"La Vie En Rose," *Get Smart*, 115
Laird, Jack, 22
Lanfield, Sidney, 38
Lansbury, Angela, 145
Larson, Jack, 2
Laugh-In, 23
Laurel, Stan, 37, 40, 41, 83
Laurel and Hardy, 70, 128
Laverne and Shirley, 136
Lawman, 47

Lazenby, George, 106
Le Carre, John, 95
Lear, Norman, 135, 136, 137, 139, 141–142, 145
Leavitt, Norman, 87
Lembeck, Harvey, 30
Leonard, Sheldon, 71, 72, 73, 83, 84
Les Miserables, 58–59
Levene, Philip, 98, 106
The Life of Riley, 124
Lindsey, George, 84
"The Little Black Book," *Get Smart*, 112
Living Alone and Loving It, 119
Logan's Run, 7
The Lone Ranger, 45–46
The Loner, 22
Long, Richard, 54
Lorre, Peter, 116
Lost, 7
"The Lost Episodes," *The Honeymooners*, 134
Love of Life, 1
Lumley, Joanna, 107
Lupino, Ida, 19
Lynch, David, 7
Lynn, Betty, 86

*M*A*S*H*, 145
Macnee, Patrick, 96, 97, 107
MacRae, Sheila, 134
Make Room for Daddy, 71
The Maltese Falcon, 111
The Man From UNCLE, 105
"The Man from Yenta," *Get Smart*, 118
"Man in a Hurry," *The Andy Griffith Show*, 86–90
Mannion, Lance, 80
Marie, Rose, 72
Marshall, Garry, 74, 78, 136
Marshall, Penny, 136
Martin, Steve, 42
Martin, Tony, 35
Martinson, Leslie, 49
Marx, Chico, 94
Marx, Groucho, 4
Marx, Harpo, 94
Marx, Zeppo, 35
Marx Brothers, 70, 94

Index

Mary Hartman, Mary Hartman, 145
Matheson, Richard, 7, 13, 21
Matlock, 92
Matthau, Walter, 127
Matthews, Larry, 72
Maude, 145
Maverick, 43, 47, 48, 52, 57, 68
Maverick, "Shady Deal at Sunny Acres." *See* "Shady Deal at Sunny Acres," *Maverick*
Maverick: Legend of the West, 48
Mayberry 101, 89
Mayberry R.F.D., 91
Maynard, Ken, 44
McHale's Navy, 25, 26, 27, 36–42, 69, 124, 140
McHale's Navy, "Dear Diary." *See* "Dear Diary," *McHale's Navy*
McHale's Navy (movie), 42
McNear, Howard, 84
McQueen, Steve, 134
Meadows, Audrey, 125
Meet Me in St. Louis, 13
Melancholia, 7
Melnick, Daniel, 108
Melvin, Allan, 30
The Merchant of Venice, 62
Meredith, Burgess, 7
Meyer, David. *See* Janssen, David
A Midsummer Night's Dream, 70
Miller, Arthur, 121
"Mission: Highly Improbable," *The Avengers*, 105
Mission: Impossible, 105
"The Monsters are Due on Maple Street," *The Twilight Zone*, 21
Montagne, Edward J., 26, 36
Montgomery, Elizabeth, 20
Moody, King, 109
Moore, Clayton, 45
Moore, Mary Tyler, 72–73, 81, 84
Moore, Roger, 57
Morris, Howard, 85
Morse, Barry, 59, 60, 64
Mostel, Zero, 35
"The Motor Pool Mardi Gras," *Bilko*, 34
Mr. Broadway, 109
Mr. Halpern and Mr. Johnson, 134

Mulholland Drive, 7
Murder, She Wrote, 145

Nabors, Jim, 84, 87
Neill, Noel, 2
Neuman, E. Jack, 19–20
"Never Bathe on Saturday," *The Dick Van Dyke Show*, 81
"Never Send a Boy King to Do a Man's Job," *The Rockford Files*, 57
The New Avengers, 107
The New Phil Silvers Show, 35
Newman, Paul, 52
Nicholson, Jack, 136
Night Gallery, 22
"Night of the Meek," *The Twilight Zone*, 5
"Nightmare at Northoak," *The Fugitive*, 59–68
Nimoy, Leonard, 7
No Time for Sergeants, 84
Noises Off, 70
North by Northwest, 58, 109
Nothing in Common, 134
The Nude Bomb, 119
Nyby, Christian, 60
Nye, Louis, 37

O'Connor, Carroll, 135, 145
O'Connor, Hugh, 145
"October Eve," *The Dick Van Dyke Show*, 81
The Odd Couple, 127, 136
"The Odyssey of Flight 33," *The Twilight Zone*, 5
The Official Dick Van Dyke Show Book, 74
The Official Honeymooners Treasury, 130
O'Hara, U.S. Treasury, 68
Oliver, Susan, 91
Olivier, Laurence, 134
On Her Majesty's Secret Service, 106
"Opie the Birdman," *The Andy Griffith Show*, 90–91
The Outer Limits, 6
Overton, Frank, 15, 60–65

Index

Paar, Jack, 4
Pantomime Quiz, 4
Papa's Delicate Condition, 134
Paris, Jerry, 73, 76
"Patterns," 8
"The Perfect Female," *The Andy Griffith Show*, 86
Perry Mason, ix
Petrie, George, 126, 129
Petticoat Junction, 91
The Phil Silvers Show, 35, 69, 72, 124. See also Bilko
The Phil Silvers Show, "The Court Martial." See "The Court Martial," *Bilko*
Picnic at Hanging Rock, 7
Pink Panther, 108
Planet of the Apes, 22
Platt, Edward, 42, 109, 119
Playhouse 90, 8
Pleshette, Suzanne, 66
Poker According to Maverick, 48
Police Surgeon, 96
Poston, Tom, 37, 108
Powell, Willliam, 108
"The Prisoner of Love," *The Andy Griffith Show*, 91
Psycho, 9
Pyle, Denver, 85

Raich, Bill, 66–67
Randolph, Joyce, 125
Raye, Martha, 28
Raynor, William, 38, 41
Rear Window, 111
Rebel Without a Cause, 109
Redford, Robert, 7, 52
Reeves, George, 1, 2
Reiner, Carl, 7, 71–72, 73, 74, 77, 81, 83, 136
Reiner, Rob, 136
Renaldo, Duncan, 45
Requiem for a Heavyweight, 8, 134
Reynolds, Burt, 7
Reynolds, Debbie, 35
Rich, John, 137
Richard Diamond, Private Detective, 58
Rickles, Don, 7, 112
The Rifleman, 47

Rigg, Diane, 95, 96, 97, 106–107, 117
Robertson, Ed, 48
The Rockford Files, 57, 68
Rogers, Roy, 44, 45
Romeo and Juliet, 60
Romero, George, 6
Rooney, Mickey, 135
Roosevelt, Eleanor, 145
Rose, Reginald, 8
Ross, Joe E., 35
Royal Shakespeare Company, 97
Rueben, Aaron, 85
Russell, A. J., 126

"The Same Pomerantz Scandals," *The Dick Van Dyke Show*, 83
Sands, Billy, 25, 139–140
Sansberry, Hope, 29–30
Sardou, 70
Satenstein, Frank, 126
Sayonara, 49
Schaeffer, Natalie, ix
Schmidt, Kim, 20
Search for Tomorrow, 1
Sellers, Peter, 108
Serling, Rod, 5, 7, 8–9, 10, 11, 12–13, 14, 15, 17–19, 21–22, 23, 134
"Seven Against the Sea," *McHale's Navy*, 36
"The Seven Faces of Ensign Parker," *McHale's Navy*, 41
"Shady Deal at Sunny Acres," *Maverick*, 49–56
Shaw, Robert, 52
Shayamalan, M. Night, 7
Sheldon, Gene, 3
Sheppard, Sam, 58
Ship of Fools, 111
Silvers, Phil, 27, 29, 35
Simon, Neil, 127
Sinatra, Frank, 27, 36
"The Sixteen-Millimeter Shrine," *The Twilight Zone*, 19
"The Sixth Sense," *The Twilight Zone*, 7
The $64,000 Question, 109
Slayer, 6
Smith, Hal, 84
Smith, Nicholas, 100

Index

Smokey and the Bandit, 134
Soldier in the Rain, 134
The Sopranos, 7
The Spy Who Came in From the Cold, 95
Stalag 17, 80
Stapleton, Jean, 135, 145
Star Trek, 6
Star Wars, 7
Steele, Bob, 44
Stern, Leonard, 109
Stevens, Craig, 109
Stevens, Robert, 9
Stewart, James, 58
The Sting, 52, 54, 57
"A Stop at Willoughby," The Twilight Zone, 19
Stritch, Elaine, 125
Struthers, Sally, 136
Stump the Stars, 4
Styler, Burt, 137, 139, 141–142
Sugarfoot, 47
Summer Stock, 27, 83
Sutton, Frank, 42
Sweeney, Bob, 86

Take Me Along, 134
"Tales from the Darkside," The Twilight Zone, 6
Talman, William, ix
Teacher's Pet, 20
Tedrow, Irene, 16
The Tempest, 49
"Ten Thousand Pieces of Silver," The Fugitive, 66
That Was the Week That Was, 108
"That's My Boy???" The Dick Van Dyke Show, 83
"There's One in Every Port," The Rockford Files, 57
They Shoot Horses, Don't They? 20
"They'll Be Some Changes Made," Get Smart, 115
"They're Tearing Down Tim Riley's Bar," The Twilight Zone, 22–23
The Thin Man, 108
The Thirty-Nine Steps, 58
Thomas, Danny, 72, 83, 84
Thorson, Linda, 107

Three Stooges, 69
Thurman, Uma, 107
Till Death Do Us Part, 136
Timeless as Infinity: The Complete "Twilight Zone" Scripts of Rod Serling, 9
"To Serve Man," The Twilight Zone, 6
To Tell the Truth, 4
The Tonight Show, 4
Toomey, Regis, 50
Top Banana, 27
Tracy, Spencer, 36
"The Transfer," Bilko, 34
"The Trouble With Templeton," The Twilight Zone, 19–20
The Truman Show, 7
The Twilight Zone, x, 5–23, 52, 143
The Twilight Zone: Unlocking the Door to a Television Classic (Martin Grams Jr.), 9
The Twilight Zone, "Walking Distance." See "Walking Distance," The Twilight Zone
Twin Peaks, 7
2001: A Space Odyssey, 7

Unger, Felix, 127
The United States Steel Hour, 84

Van Dyke, Dick, 41, 71–72, 73–74, 83, 92
Vertigo, 9
Vidal, Gore, 8, 20

Waiting for Godot, 30
Waldron, Vince, 74
The Walking Dead, 6
"Walking Distance," The Twilight Zone, x, 5, 7, 8, 9–19, 20, 21, 23
The Waltons, 7
Warren, Brooks, and Chapin, "You Wonderful You," 83
Wayne, John, 46
Weil, Joseph "Yellow Kid," 49
Weird Tales, 8
Welles, Orson, 134
What's My Line, 4
Who Do You Trust? 72
"Who Shot J.R.," Dallas, 67

Index

"Who's Who," *The Avengers*, 106
Wiard, William, 111
Wickwire, Nancy, 60–65
Wilder, Billy, 80
Wilder, Miles, 38, 41
"Will the Real Martian Please Stand Up," *The Twilight Zone*, 6
William Tell (Rossini), 46
Williams, Guy, 3
"The Winged Avenger," *The Avengers*, 105–106
"A World of His Own," *The Twilight Zone*, 21–22
Wyatt Earp, 47

Wynn, Ed, 7
Wynn, Keenan, 21

The X Files, 7

You Bet Your Life, 4
"You Wonderful You," 83
You'll Never Get Rich, 35. See also *The Phil Silvers Show*
Young, Gig, 7, 9, 10, 16, 20, 21
Your Show of Shows, 71, 85, 108

Zimbalist, Jr., Efrem, 54
Zorro, 2, 3, 47

About The Author

Victor L. Cahn is Professor Emeritus of English at Skidmore College, where he taught courses in Shakespeare, modern drama, the history of drama, and expository writing.

He has written five books on Shakespeare, including *Shakespeare the Playwright: A Companion to the Complete Tragedies, Histories, Comedies, and Romances* (named an Outstanding Academic Book by *Choice*); critical volumes on Tom Stoppard and Harold Pinter; *Conquering College*; the memoir *Classroom Virtuoso*; *Polishing Your Prose* (with Steven M Cahn); and two novels, *Romantic Trapezoid* and *Sound Bites*. His articles and reviews have appeared in such varied publications as *Modern Drama, The Literary Review, The Chronicle of Higher Education, The New York Times,* and *Variety*.

Dr. Cahn is the author of many plays, several of which have been produced Off-Broadway and in regional theater: *Roses in December, Embraceable Me, Fit to Kill* (all published by Samuel French), *Dally with the Devil* (Steele Spring Stage Rights), *A Dish for the Gods, Getting the Business, Sheepskin/Bottom of the Ninth,* and *Sherlock Solo*, a one-man show that he performs. Other scripts have been presented throughout the Capital Region of New York, where he has taken leading roles in works by Shakespeare, Shaw, Pinter, Ayckbourn, Coward, Simon, Gurney, and Knott.

www.ingramcontent.com/pod-product-compliance
Lightning Source LLC
Chambersburg PA
CBHW051104160426
43193CB00010B/1305